14-
5/2

Treasury of
AMERICAN ANTIQUES

Treasury of
AMERICAN ANTIQUES

A Pictorial Survey of Popular
Folk Arts & Crafts

—◆—

Clarence P. Hornung

HARRY N. ABRAMS, INC., *Publishers*, NEW YORK

FRONTISPIECE

1 *The art and skill of the wood-carver are seen in this collection of ships' figureheads, carrousel animals, cigar-store Indians, and other colorful trade characters dating from the last half of the nineteenth century. Photograph by Arnold Newman, courtesy the Smithsonian Institution, Washington, D.C.*

The design as well as the text of this volume is the work of Clarence P. Hornung, who also created the typographic format. The type is set in Times Roman with initial letters in the author's Georgian initials; the chapter headings were hand-set by him in Caslon italic swash letters

Library of Congress Cataloging in Publication Data
Hornung, Clarence Pearson.
    Treasury of American antiques.
    Concise ed. of the author's Treasury of American design originally published in 2 v. in 1972.
    1. Art industries and trade—United States.
2. Design, Decorative—United States. 3. Antiques —United States. I. Title.
NK805.H67   1977   745.4'49'73   76-49914
ISBN 0-8109-1670-3
ISBN 0-8109-2060-3 pbk.

Library of Congress Catalogue Card Number: 76-49914
Published in 1977 by HARRY N. ABRAMS, INC., NEW YORK

Contents

Foreword

A S WE ENTER OUR THIRD CENTURY as a nation, Americans, more than ever, are coming to appreciate their past and the things that gave beauty and comfort to the homes and environment of their ancestors. During the early years of independence, Americans were concerned largely with the crucial problems of building a strong and vital government, and little thought was given to such amenities as the decorative arts. By the Centennial in 1876, however, interest in this long-neglected part of our heritage had begun to grow. *Harper's New Monthly Magazine* reported: "The thoughts of our people are eagerly turned . . . to a more familiar observation of the men and women who were actors in that great event [the Revolution] . . . to take note of their appearance, manners, and customs; to cross their thresholds, and see . . . what entered into their domestic appointments and belongings."

In the decades following the Centennial Exposition, it became the fashion to take a fresh look at the country's past, and for the first time the term "Early American" crept into the vocabulary of art, furnishings, and architecture. Private patrons, antiquarians, and museums began in earnest to assemble collections of the decorative and domestic art of the Colonial and Federal periods. The skillful craftsmanship of our forefathers and the beautiful objects they created were finally recognized.

The very magnitude of the world of American antiques is a challenge to anyone trying to present a representative pictorial selection in a slender volume. From the nearly three thousand illustrations in my *Treasury of American Design* I have attempted to make a selection that highlights American taste in the decorative arts, to choose those subjects which would have the broadest appeal, to offer something of interest for anyone with a curiousity about antiques. Included are sections dealing with the American eagle, figureheads, tobacconists' figures, glassware, chairs, cabinets, chests, clocks, jars and jugs, crocks and churns, stoneware, toleware, hatboxes, quilts and coverlets, hooked rugs, circus wagons, carousel figures, toys, dolls and puppets, penny coin banks, and weathervanes. The illustrations are largely from the fine colorplates in the Index of American Design at the National Gallery of Art in Washington, D.C. The Index, which consists of some seventeen thousand watercolor renderings of American crafts and folk arts, was produced by hundreds of artists throughout the country from 1935 to 1941 under the Works Progress Administration. For this invaluable record of achievement in the arts, we gratefully acknowledge our indebtedness.

C. P. H.

Treasury of
AMERICAN ANTIQUES

Symbols *of Freedom*

3

EFORE THE AMERICAN colonies became independent, on festive occasions, when custom called for a display of colors, the Union Jack was unfurled and images of Britannia were in evidence. With the Revolutionary War and the Declaration of Independence, these symbols of English domination were, of course, abandoned: the new republic required its own official emblems, a flag and a state seal.

On June, 14, 1777, Congress adopted a new flag, but various flags were used during the Revolutionary War. For example, beneath a banner of crimson and silver with the legend "Conquer or Die!" the embattled farmers at Concord Bridge fired "the shot heard round the world"; beneath the Pine Tree banner the battle of Bunker Hill was lost and won, and beneath the Rattlesnake flag the American fleet won its first victory. Hence, to sever the last link that bound the Colonies individually to England, the Stars and Stripes was created as a symbol of national unity. The thirteen red and white stripes, one for each of the states, had been a feature of an earlier flag that included the Union Jack in the upper left-hand quadrant, but the resolution on the design for the new flag replaced the small Union Jack motif with thirteen white stars, symbolizing a new constellation. (These stars were usually arranged in a circle, but placement varied.) It was this flag that represented the new country when Lord Cornwallis surrendered in 1781, and it had already become

such an accepted symbol that it was displayed widely and figured importantly in paintings, carvings, needlecraft, and metalwork.

The Stars and Stripes, along with the Great Seal and the American eagle, provided artists, designers, and craftsmen with emblems that have been used for almost two centuries. The eagle, whose use as a symbol descended from antiquity, proved a particularly versatile decorative motif. Without studying, much less submitting to, the artistic conventions governing heraldry, American artists and craftsmen intuitively recognized that there were few limits to the decorative potential of the newly adopted national symbol. Thus a profusion of decorative eagles appeared from the time of the War of 1812 through the Civil War.

Other popular patriotic emblems included the figures of Columbia and Uncle Sam—the former a poetic, the latter a comic, symbol of the United States—and of Liberty, the Liberty Bell, Independence Hall, and likenesses of George Washington.

During the closing years of the eighteenth century and the first decades of the nineteenth, artists and craftsmen used these national symbols to express the period's patriotic fervor. In the works of folk artists these motifs were given a fresh and earthy vitality. More, perhaps, than in any other period of American history, such folk works seem to spring directly from the heart and thus are exceptionally effective expressions of the ideals of freedom and unity.

4

2 General Washington on a White Charger, *painted by an unknown artist in New York, c. 1830. National Gallery of Art, Washington, D.C. Gift of Edgar William and Bernice Chrysler Garbisch* **3** *Cast-iron Liberty Bell coin banks produced at the time of the great Philadelphia Centennial in 1876* **4** *Statue of Liberty coin bank, a type very popular following the statue's unveiling in New York harbor in 1886*

5

6

7

8

12

JIM McDIVIT GLOUCESTER

5 *Carved eagle in which natural proportions have been sacrificed to emphasize head, beak, and talons* 6 *Sheet-brass powder horn displaying elaborate military motif. Late eighteenth century* 7 *Painted cast-iron mirror frame topped by an eagle. Patriotic motifs include flags, shield, officer in medallion, 1862* 8 *Carved and painted pine sea chest, combining maritime symbols—anchor and fisherman's head—with patriotic motif of eagle and shield. Made in Massachusetts, c. 1840* 9 *Stamped sheet-brass eagle, used as decoration on parade floats and platforms, 1840–50* 10 *Columbia weather vane with thirty-two-star flag. Made of cast zinc, sheet copper, and brass, c. 1865* 11 *Painted eagle appears on many regimental drums of Civil War vintage*

The Eagle Spreads Its Wings

THE EAGLE HAS long been the most popular American motif in the decorative arts and crafts. Thousands of artists and craftsmen have interpreted its image. Soaring and circling far above the earth, plunging like a meteor from the sky, screaming defiance at a storm, or fiercely striking its prey—to men of every age the eagle has embodied freedom and power. This image has been emblazoned on the chariots of warriors and on the shields of knights from the time of Caesar to the battle of Iwo Jima.

A bald-headed eagle of the American species with outspread wings and legs is prominently displayed on the Great Seal of the United States, which was approved by Congress on June 20, 1782. The use of the bird followed ancient precedents. Three thousand years before Christ the eagle had been guardian deity of Mesopotamia and had also represented Babylonia, depicted in a pose similar to that on the Great Seal.

The eagle on the Great Seal was by no means the first emblematic eagle to make its appearance in the American Colonies. As early as 1700, one was stamped on a New York token of lead or brass; in 1776 it was featured on a Massachusetts copper penny within a semicircle of thirteen stars; and in 1778 the State of New York included an eagle perched on a globe as part of its official coat of arms. However, the eagle of the Great Seal is the first specified as being of the American bald-headed species, "bald" in the older sense of the term, meaning white.

A bald-headed American eagle was also incorporated in a design by Major l'Enfant for a badge for the Society of Cincinnati, a group founded in 1783 by members of the American revolutionary army. Benjamin Franklin, although well-informed in a wide variety of fields, was apparently no ornithologist, and on seeing the badge, he wrote to his daughter from France: "I am, on this account, not displeased that the figure is not

12 Eagle signboard with the owner's name, J. Procter, hung outside the entrance to the Red Lion Inn at Red Lion, Delaware. Washington is known to have stopped here, for an entry in his diary for March 1791 notes that he gave his horses "a bite of Hay at the Red Lyon" on his way to Mount Vernon. Photograph courtesy the Henry Francis du Pont Winterthur Museum, Winterthur, Delaware   13 Painted pine eagle clutching arrows and shield. Carved by Samuel McIntire in 1805. From the customhouse at Salem   14 Pine sternboard eagle with foliated scrolls or rinceaux. Early nineteenth century

14

15

16

LOUISVILLE KY

18

16

17

19

20

15 *Carved pine eagle, probably made in Newport, Rhode Island, c. 1830* 16 *Ribbed whisky flask with eagle in oval. Made by Louisville, Kentucky, glassworks* 17 *Cast-brass eagle, mounted on an acorn-shaped walnut base* 18 *Pine eagle, nearly five feet tall, said to have served as a signboard for an unidentified ''Eagle Tavern'' in Rhode Island. Feathers on breast, wings, and back, individually cut in high relief, reveal powerful carving, c. 1850–75. Photograph courtesy Colonial Williamsburg* 19 *Ceramic eagle used as a mantel decoration* 20 *Snare drum of bent wood with painted eagle, mid-nineteenth century* 21 *Coverlet with woven design including eagle, the most popular motif in the first half of the nineteenth century*

21

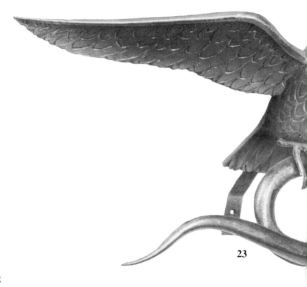

22

23

24

known as a bald eagle but looks more like a turkey. For in truth, the turkey is in comparison a much more respectable bird and withal a true original native of America. Eagles have been found in all countries, but the turkey is peculiar to ours. . . . He is, besides, (though a little vain and silly, it is true, but not the worse emblem for that) a bird of courage, and would not hesitate to attack a grenadier of the British guards, who should presume to invade his farmyard with a red coat on." In the preceding paragraph Franklin had expressed the wish that "the bald eagle had not been chosen

25

22 *Eagle weather vane, nineteenth century. Photograph courtesy the Smithsonian Institution, Washington, D.C.*   **23** *Gilded wood eagle and snake, nineteenth century*   **24** *Carved eagle with shield and arrows. Photograph courtesy the Smithsonian Institution, Washington, D.C.*   **25** *Cast-iron eagle flagpole holder, 1856*   **26** *Carved eagle ornament. Photograph courtesy the Smithsonian Institution, Washington, D.C.*   **27** *Carved eagle figurehead, early nineteenth century*   **28** *Cast-iron eagle desk ornament*   **29** *Eagle with realistically detailed feathers and proportions revealing a strong Napoleonic influence, especially in the bolts of lightning clutched by the talons*

18

26

27

28

29

as the representative of our country; he is a bird of bad moral character; he does not get his living honestly . . . too lazy to fish for himself, he watches the labor of the fishing-hawk, and when that diligent bird has at length taken a fish, and is bearing it to his nest for the support of his mate and his young ones, the bald eagle pursues him and takes it from him . . . like those men who live by sharping and robbing he is generally poor, and often very lousy. Besides he is a rank coward; the little king-bird, not bigger than a sparrow, attacks him boldly and drives him out of the district."

After the adoption of the Great Seal, a variety of eagles appeared on other seals and insignia, including those for departments of the federal and state governments and the presidential seal, and on coins. Frequently, as on the presidential seal, the eagle turns its head to the left, whereas on the Great Seal the head turns toward the right, which is considered the correct position. Other variations include placing arrows in the right claw and the olive branch in the left, reducing the number of arrows or of stripes in the shield, and placing the eagle on the shield instead of the shield on the eagle. Some people condemn these revisions for not conforming to heraldic law.

Various eagles, especially those on coins, have also been criticized for being of alien breed, for example, for having the long feathered trousers characteristic of the golden eagle; whereas the American eagle, except in its juvenal stage, has bare or half-bare shanks, extremely conspicuous because they are bright yellow.

With appropriate democratic impartiality, the eagle lent itself to the decoration of porcelain dinner services—which were imported from England and China because an American porcelain industry was slow to develop but which used American motifs—and kitchen crockery. It was impressed into whisky flasks and Sandwich glass, woven into curtain and upholstery fabrics, and perched as a finial on mirrors, clocks, and weather vanes. It was carved into butter stamps and delicately inlaid in drawing-room furniture, painted on tavern signs and cast into flatiron holders, and even stitched in quilted counterpanes, complete with arrows, olive branch, scroll, and overhead stars. The eagle was also minted in a number of forms, but its image on coins and paper money is not nearly as varied as are its manifestations on other types of objects.

The most interesting and beautiful eagles are found among those carved in wood, ei-

32

ther in relief or in the round, as decorative panels for sofas, chairs, and mantelpieces; over the doorways of public buildings or private dwellings; on cupolas and gateposts; as shop or tavern signs; or as figureheads. This medium—mahogany and pine were the preferred woods—attracted both self-taught folk artists and trained sculptors, architects, and cabinetmakers. Fine marquetry eagles were inlaid in mahogany, satinwood, and maple chests, slant-top and tambour desks, secretaries, tall clocks, knife boxes, and tilt-top tables. The number of inlaid stars in a piece was usually the same as the number of states in the Union at the time, which helps to date the piece.

First among the untrained craftsmen was the Pennsylvania German whittler Wilhelm Schimmel, who worked during the post-Civil War years. Of the academicians, one of the most distinguished was America's first native-born sculptor, William Rush (1756–1833), among whose surviving works are two magnificent eagles carved as emblems, one for a church and the other for a fire company.

Samuel McIntire, born a year after Rush, has been called the most celebrated of the craftsmen-architects of America. He was fond of making an eagle in relief against a background of stars the central motif of his exquisite mantelpieces, and of cresting the rails of his equally beautiful mahogany sofas with the emblem. He also executed eagles in the round with closed wings and eagles perched on globes as ornaments for gate arches and cupolas. Among his works is a noble spread eagle which was placed over the door of the Old Custom House in his native Salem. McIntire's New York contemporary, Duncan Phyfe, like other cabinetmakers of the period, made charming mahogany chairs with eagle splats for distinguished clients.

In retrospect, it seems fortunate that the founding fathers chose the eagle, which could be easily rendered and interpreted in most mediums in a great variety of attitudes—perching, preening, soaring, gliding, attacking, and alighting. For the versatility of our national symbol has continued to inspire countless artists and artisans.

30–33 *The spread eagle took many forms, with and without accessory decorations, as a motif ideally suited to the stern of a ship. The horizontal extension of the wings varied from five to eight feet. In contrast to the figurehead at the bow, which called for treatment in the round, sternboard eagles were executed in comparatively low relief. Coupled with the eagle were such design elements as flags, drapes, the shield, and the ribbon bearing the motto* E Pluribus Unum. *A fine example of gilded pine carved by Alton Skillin for the U.S.S.* Enterprise *in 1881 is shown in 30. The eagle and shield in 31 were carved by John Bellamy*

33

Forgotten Figures, Fore & Aft

35

36

IN COLONIAL TIMES, shipbuilding was vital to maintaining the lifeline between America and England. The industry began in 1607, when the thirty-two-ton pinnace *Virginia* was built at the mouth of the Kennebec River in Maine. The next thirteen years saw only occasional construction of some small craft; but in 1620 the Virginia Company —realizing that this slow progress meant the hiring of foreign hulls, which would considerably diminish profits—decided to import twenty-five professional shipwrights from England. Within eight years, the colony of Massachusetts Bay welcomed a group of six ship carpenters. Similar steps were taken by the French in Canada, the Dutch in New Amsterdam, the Swedes in Delaware, and the English in other ports along the eastern seaboard. By about 1700 the American merchant fleet numbered some fifteen hundred vessels, most of which made their home port in Boston and nearby waters.

After 1776 our native carvers, who made their headquarters in the major shipbuilding centers—near the waterfront of India Wharf in Boston, on South Street in New York, or on Front Street in Philadelphia—needed a new vocabulary to express their new-found spirit of independence. The British lion, the coiled serpent, or the fire-breathing dragon gave way to the proud eagle. The figures of Miss Liberty and Columbia replaced the mythological gods and goddesses. Figures of presidents and statesmen, characters from literature and history, as well as ordinary men and women, were placed at the bow.

The carving of figureheads was a highly skilled craft, the training for which was rooted in the old guild system of master, journeyman, and apprentice. The length of the apprentice's service depended upon how quickly he learned and his value in the shop. Most figurehead carvers whose names have come down to us served an apprenticeship and in turn trained eager youngsters. A list of more than seven hundred carvers has been compiled and authenticated, and, as research continues, more names will undoubtedly be added.

The attitude, size, and position of a ship's figurehead was determined by the limited space under the bowsprit. The early figureheads were almost perpendicular to the water line, whereas in the clipper-ship era the angle of the bowsprit and the water line, and thus of the figurehead, was acute.

The specifications for the figurehead some-

34 Figurehead, carved of oak, from the American barque Edinburgh, *by John Rogerson, 1883* **35** *Three-quarter-length figure from the clipper ship* Rhine, *c. 1850* **36** *Female bust surmounting scroll and acanthus leaves to form a terminal for the bow of a ship, c. 1790*

37

38

times required that it measure as much as eight feet in height and at least three feet in diameter at its widest point. The mechanical problems presented by such requirements were solved quite ingeniously. Since no single tree trunk could be found which was sufficiently large to enable the carving to be done from a single piece, the block was built from many smaller sections and then carefully joined together by means of trunnels (wooden pegs). The pieces had to be studied to make certain that the grain always ran in the same direction to prevent splintering and facilitate the carving of details.

If a plan called for a figure with outstretched arms, rather than search the forest for a satisfactory trunk and limbs, it was more practical to carve the arms separately and dowel them to the main body with dovetail slip joints. Sometimes these outstretched arms were detachable to avoid damage by storms. They could be removed when the vessel left port and replaced

37 Unusually realistic modeling distinguishes this formally gowned female figure from the sloop Postmaster **38** Three-quarter-length figure posed in an attitude popular with ship carvers, c. 1840 **39** Elegantly costumed girl with flowers from the Creole, built in 1847 **40** Female tar holding straw sailor hat and an oar and gowned in Classic costume with finely scrolled bodice, c. 1850

41

42

43 *American ship carvers were at their best when modeling the female figure* **44** *The Classical pose is based on the marble statue of Artemis at Versailles; from the ship* Cassandra Adams, *built in 1876*

43

44

before it entered the next harbor. When ships were eventually broken up for salvage and their fittings sold, arms and other parts of the figureheads were often lost, and many a full-length figure was turned into a three-quarter-length one or truncated torso. Many of the surviving figures now on view at museums take on the appearance of *Venus de Milo*.

One of the great names among American carvers is that of Samuel McIntire (1757-1811) of Salem, Massachusetts. McIntire was also a trained architect and cabinetmaker. The homes he built in Salem, many of which can still be seen today, attest to his skill, taste, and versatility. By virtue of his technical background, he was a precise and meticulous craftsman,

45 *Mid-nineteenth-century female bust* **46** *This head, with its extreme forward thrust, avoids the static pose of upright figures* **47** *Decorative effect in this female portrait bust is enhanced by hairdo, jewelry, and supporting structure* **48** *Ornamental details of coiffure, dress trimmings, and scroll enrich this female figure* **49** *Forward motion is strongly suggested in the attitude of this head* **50** *Half-length figure from the whaler* Marcia, *built in 1832, suggests Classical inspiration* **51** *Unusual drapery treatment characterizes this half-length figure* **52** *A type of female figurehead that was a great favorite with sailors*

49

50

51

52

29

53

54

exhibiting none of the spontaneous traits of the folk artist. Today we have only one piece of ship carving that can be ascribed to McIntire, although many of his sketches and designs for stern decorations have been preserved. Many eagle figureheads were undoubtedly his handiwork; they exhibit characteristics similar to those seen in the fine detailing of his architectural decorations.

John Bellamy (1836–1914), a carver who had a shop at Kittery, Maine, across the river from the busy seaport of Portsmouth, New Hamp-

53 *From the* Indian Chief *that sailed out of Salem, this realistically painted tribesman is among the finest native Americans to ride the waves* **54** *Two-faced Janus, probably from a ship of that name* **55** *The carver of this figurehead sought inspiration from an ancient Roman statue. Detailing of the head and facial features shows greater competence than does the handling of the drapery folds* **56** *In this unique composition an aboriginal bust tops the acanthus scrolls of the billethead* **57** *Male figurehead, probably intended to glorify the shipowner* **58** *Typical of many heavily draped female figures that adorned the bows of ships in the mid-nineteenth century*

55

shire, is famed for glorifying our national symbol, the American eagle. He made hundreds of fine eagles for the navy and commercial shipbuilders, each bearing his unmistakable marks: finely chiseled head and beak, stylized feather forms, and concave wings often adorned with flowing ribbons, pennants, and shields. Bellamy's masterpiece is the gigantic (eighteen-foot wingspread) eagle for the U.S.S. *Lancaster*, now at the Mariners' Museum, Newport News, Virginia.

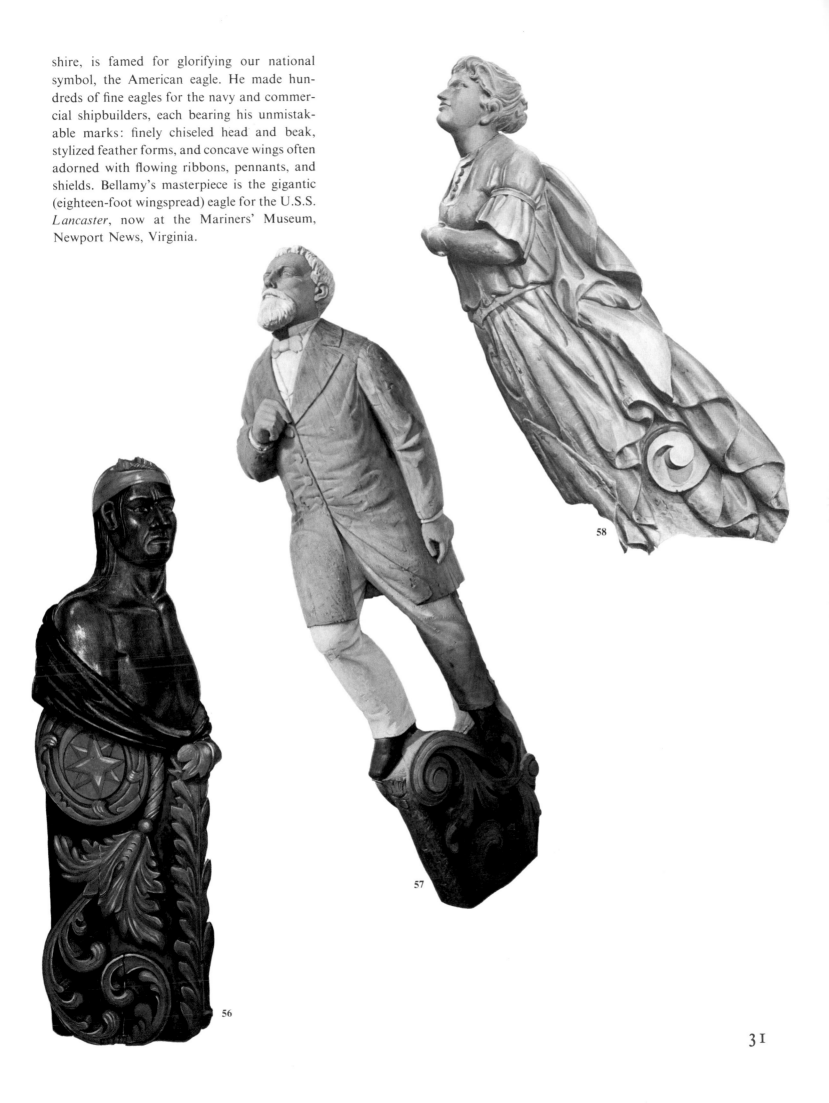

56

57

58

59

60

The Tobacconists' Tribe

T RADESMAN'S SIGNS and symbols, designed as eye-catchers to lure the passerby into shop or tavern, have been with us as long as recorded history. The familiar barber pole, whose spiraling red and white stripes originated in the Middle Ages, the pawnbroker's sign of three balls, the hanging shoe to mark the cobbler's shop, and the watch to show the jeweler's establishment—all indicate the power of symbols over words. The earliest American signs are also interesting visual reminders of how branded merchandise, which has so strongly molded our present-day buying habits, had its humble origins.

Carved wooden figures of tradesmen existed in the Colonies as early as 1720, when there appeared a shop figure of a short, stocky gentleman clad in blue coat, red vest, knee breeches, and buckled shoes. His belt, which is inscribed "1720," shows that he antedates by more than a half century the ubiquitous cigar-

store Indians who later proclaimed the tobacconist's wares.

When and where the first cigar-store figure appeared has not been accurately determined. Well-founded conjecture seems to point to a London tobacconist's shop early in the eighteenth century, when the growing habit of taking snuff brought prosperity to the tobacco trade. (Tobacco did not become an important article of commerce until long after Sir Walter Raleigh introduced it into England by way of the Colonies, and snuff could only be bought in an apothecary shop.) With the establishment of the Virginia plantations and the West Indies trade, the tobacco habit caught on, and many retail shops were opened during the reign of Queen Anne.

At this time the first wooden Indians in England, used to designate tobacco shops, were called "black boys" because of their resemblance to the young black slaves imported to her colonies from Jamaica. It may

61

59 *Indian princess wearing a costume typical of the cigar-store Indian: feather headdress and girdle and a fringed buckskin tunic, to which a beaded necklace and metal breastplate add color. In her right hand she holds a plug of tobacco and in her left, a bunch of cigars* **60** *In contrast to the mild-mannered face of the squaw, there was often a suggestion of ferocity in the face of a chieftain* **61** *Modeling of the face and headdress represented the carver's greatest opportunity to demonstrate his skill*

33

62

63

CIGARS
TOBACCO

C.H. MANLEY & CO.
INDUSTRY CIGARS

64

J.M. ANTHONY
-CIGARS-

62–73 *The variety of wooden Indian types was greatly influenced by the romantic image created in popular nineteenth-century prints, engravings, and lithographs, and especially by the novels of James Fenimore Cooper. Indian tribes such as the Pequot and the Iroquois of New England, the Shawnee and Chippewa of the Midwest, and the Shoshoni and Navajo farther west contributed to the iconographic lore available to the carvers. Documentation on these figures is vague; rarely is the date or maker's name known. Although they were made from about 1850 to the*

PONY
AVIATOR

65

66

67

68

69

70

close of the century, it is generally agreed that the carving of tobacconists' Indians reached its peak in the 1890s. Some cast-metal figures appeared in the late eighties; they were expensive but, because of their weight, were not as easily stolen as the wooden Indians. Figure 71 is of cast zinc, with a wrought-iron bow. The heroic pose of the chieftain returning from the hunt (66) is unique

71

72

73

74

75

76

74–85 *The popular image created by the carvers in their female figures was a glorified version of the Indian maiden—a stereotype that bore little resemblance to reality. The chubby characters depicted in 75 and 78 depend solely upon headdress and costume for their Indian identity. The shapely squaws in 79 and 84, wearing belted*

77

78

79

80

81

82

dresses and high-button shoes, were not to be found in Indian villages. Occasionally, the squaw was depicted carrying her papoose (81). An unusual pose (76) shows a squaw with crossed legs. The position with the left leg resting on an extra block (85) may be traced to the influence of ship carvers

83

84

85

37

be that these wooden figures were never intended to represent Indians at all, for the tobacco industry in America depended heavily on the work of slaves imported from Africa.

As the tobacco trade between the United States and Britain grew, British retailing and merchandising techniques were introduced to American tobacconists. The "black boy" became a full-blooded American Indian, starting a clan whose progeny were to dot the streets of American towns and villages. As the smoking of "segars" by men grew more popular, thousands of retail shops sprang up, each displaying some form of wooden Indian. Many of these figures were permanently bolted into position at the shopfront; others were mounted on wheels so that they could be rolled in at night, because vandals singled out these Indians as special targets.

Tobacconist figures fall into four categories: Chiefs, Squaws or Pocahontases, Blackamoors or Pompeys, and White Men. Indians, both

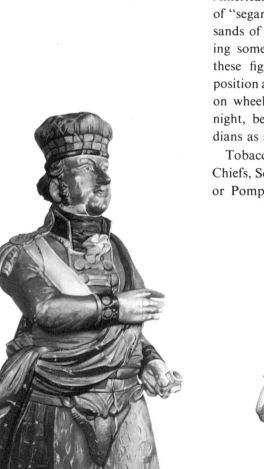

86 *In shops where numbers of cigar-store figures were carved, the trade term "White Men" was used to designate figures other than Indians. This figure, called "The Dude," was made about 1890* **87** *Highland chief, in tartan kilt, bonnet, brown jacket with gold epaulettes, and fur sporran with animal's head, may have marked the shop of a Scottish tobacconist*

male and female, predominated, and thus the term "cigar-store Indian" became the generic name for all types of tobacconist figures. Chiefs appeared in a variety of dress and headgear, including the fully dressed Seminole type with plumed headdress as seen in George Catlin's portrait of Osceola. Braves were also divided into categories: an Indian with his hand shading his eyes was a "scout"; one holding a gun or bow and arrow was a "hunting chief"; if his head was shaved except for the scalp lock, he was a "Captain Jack."

The White Men, so called to distinguish them from Red Men, included Scots; British officers with high bearskin shakos or small fatigue caps; heavy swells of Civil War days with long, flowing side whiskers (called dundrearies) and generously wide trousers; Dolly Vardens in skirts with panniers and hats tilted forward on high headdresses; Punches with the hooked nose, protuberant chin, and hump; Columbines with skirts alarmingly short for

91

89

90

88 *Belle of the 1890s with lower limbs displayed and skirt uplifted represented a daring departure in its day* **89** *Scotchman in tartan kilt offers a pinch of snuff to the passerby* **90** *Figure of Judy dressed as a clown, with smiling painted face and turned-in toes* **91** *Punch, with jovial expression and gay attitude, wearing a cornucopia hat and clown's outfit with a ruff*

39

the times. The list also includes the conventional plantation Negro with a wide expanse of shirt collar; grave Turks and sultanas; Yankee Doodle; Columbia; warlike Zouaves and other American Civil War types, such as cavalrymen; gallants of the period sporting Prince Albert cutaways and marvelous pantaloons; racetrack touts and Bowery belles equipped with bustles in the height of fashion; baseball players; sailors; firemen; policemen; and even sculptured likenesses of the shop proprietors.

The heyday of the Indian passed with the nineties. Changing fashions and current events fired the carvers with fresh inspiration. There was an outburst of dudes and dandies, and at the time of the Spanish-American War, Rough Riders and statues of Admiral Dewey became popular.

The closing years of the nineteenth century witnessed a gradual decline in the production of wooden figures. New ordinances by meddlesome local governments branded them traffic obstructions and ordered them off the sidewalks. One by one they were hauled inside, where they lost their original purpose; some were carted off to city junkheaps or consigned to log piles for firewood. From an estimated total of about seventy-five thousand, the tribe has now dwindled to a handful of survivors. The wooden Indian, like his prototype, has been put on a reservation—in his case an honored spot in a museum or a treasured position in a private collection. *Requiescat in pace!*

92–95 *Just as the tobacconists adopted the Indian to symbolize cigars and snuff, mid-nineteenth-century tea shops and importers used the Chinaman and Oriental women to advertise goods imported from the Orient* **96** *Carved figure holding a bunch of grapes, probably used in a wine merchant's shop* **97** *Military and naval men were among the figures used on shop fronts; this one, c. 1870* **98** *Ship chandlers and instrument shops used figures like this to symbolize their trade* **99** *Female figure, probably used in a women's apparel or millinery shop* **100** *Unique among eighteenth-century signboards is this manacled felon (c. 1775) that was placed over the door of a jail in East Greenwich, Rhode Island, serving as a warning that "crime does not pay"* **101** *Minstrel or house servant, used outside a tavern to welcome wayfarers*

96

97

98

99

100

101

Gleaming Glassware for Table & Buffet

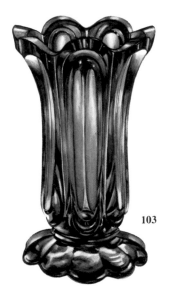

103

GLASSMAKING HAS BEEN a highly honored craft since the days of the ancient Egyptians. During the Middle Ages, the craft guilds emphasized the mysteries surrounding the glassmaking process. To the layman, the making of glass seemed to involve a sorcerer's alchemy, in which a rigid, transparent substance could be created by fusing a composite of opaque inert materials, such as sand, soda, lime, and lead, at high temperatures and then cooling the resulting liquid. Various luminous colors could be produced by adding metallic oxides to this liquid, which could be blown or cast in molds, or drawn or rolled into fine threads of gossamer delicacy.

A few glassmakers came to America from European factories when the Colonies were first established, lured by promises of profit sharing in exchange for assisting in the founding of new factories. Although passage and subsistence were assured, the workers' jobs were often short-lived, and they found themselves lost in an alien environment with meager resources.

In 1608 a small group of Dutch and Polish glassmakers were invited to the colony of Jamestown, Virginia, by John Smith, who had observed that there was a plentiful supply of the necessary raw materials in the Virginia countryside. But the enterprise did not prosper and the group soon dispersed.

The first successful glass manufactory was established in 1739 by Caspar Wistar on the banks of Alloway's Creek in southern New Jersey, not far from Philadelphia. Wistar, a German, had come to the Colonies as a young man in 1717. He was a manufacturer of brass buttons, but envisioned an unlimited potential in the glass business. He brought over four "glass experts" from Germany, and thus Early American blown glass was influenced by German styles. Wistar died in 1752, but his son Richard carried on the business until after the Revolutionary War.

This glassware was for the most part free

104

102 *American glass made c. 1770 to 1850. The pattern-molded blue covered sugar bowl with spiral finial, the engraved covered tumbler, and the lily-pad decorated sugar bowl whose cover is topped by a chicken finial are representative of the three major traditions of American glassware that developed in the eighteenth century: the Stiegel, the Amelung, and the South Jersey. The pattern-molded pocket bottles and cruet are characteristic of Midwestern glasshouses of the 1815–40 era, while the mold-blown sugar bowl, decanter, and creamer represent the beginnings of American mass-produced glass, Photograph courtesy Corning Museum of Glass, Corning, New York* 103 *Thick-walled tulip pattern Sandwich glass celery holder with petalous base, c. 1840–50* 104 *Vase with loop pattern bowl, goffered rim, and hexagonal shaft on a square plinth*

105

106

107

blown, which means that it was manipulated and shaped in the technique which has been practiced for centuries by Italians, Germans, Swiss, Dutchmen, and Bohemians. The glass gather (a mass of molten glass) is worked at just the right temperature, being blown and rotated at the same time. The blower reheats the glass when necessary, judging the temperature by color and pliability.

Henry William Stiegel, like Wistar, came to the Colonies from Germany. He arrived in 1750 at the age of twenty-one and settled near Lancaster, Pennsylvania. He soon found employment with Jacob Huber, master of a pioneer ironworks, and within two years married Huber's daughter Elizabeth. After several years in the iron business, Stiegel

105 *Open-necked blown amber vase with swirled ribbing*
106 *Stiegel-type blown-glass footed sugar bowl with lid, c. 1770*
107 *Flip glass or runner, with enameled decoration and familiar bird motif used by Stiegel* **108** *Sugar bowl and cover; pattern molded in ogival design with swirl finial* **109** *Footed bowl with folded rim and swirled ribbing, a pattern-molded salt of the late eighteenth century* **110** *Heavy, footed eight-sided goblet, with enameled decoration showing strong influence of German and Bohemian styles*

108

109

decided to go into glassmaking. In 1763 he built his first glasshouse, near the ironworks. By 1769 he had established two more at Manheim, a town he had founded and where he indulged in a baronial manner of living reminiscent of the German aristocracy. At this point "Baron Stiegel," as he called himself, employed a hundred and thirty people.

As the nation grew, there was a great increase in the number of successful glass factories. By 1820 there were some forty glass factories in operation; by 1830 this number had increased to about ninety, with new firms constantly entering the field.

At Sandwich, Massachusetts, Deming Jarves produced the first drinking vessel made by means of a glass-pressing device. As happens with the introduction of many new labor-saving processes, Jarves's workers were infuriated at the prospect of being thrown out of work.

Most manufacturers of table glassware adopted, rather freely, whatever pattern caught the public's fancy. When patternmakers were not busy inventing new designs, they were busy copying those of their competitors. Thus, it is difficult to trace a particular pattern to a specific source.

110

46

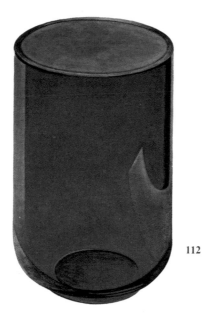

112

Goblets & Tumblers

RINKING GLASSES vary in size, purpose, and color. They can be plain or decorated, footed or stemmed, and so on, and there are many lesser classifications. They fall into two major divisions, tumblers and goblets.

A tumbler is a straight-sided drinking glass without a handle, stem, or foot. Originally, it had a convex or pointed base, and could not stand upright, hence the name tumbler. A tumbler of liquid was served in a tray of sand to keep it in an upright position. The liquid was taken at a single draft and then the tumbler was placed on the table with its bottom up, thus the expression "bottoms up." Most whisky glasses are of the tumbler variety. A large tumbler with a ten-ounce capacity was called a flip glass. Flips were made in plain clear transparent glass, either cut, blown, or pressed, and engraved or enameled.

The term "goblet" applies to a drinking glass of any ovoid or globular bowl shape, supported on a stem. Cocktail glasses are usually tall stemmed; wine glasses or cordial glasses vary greatly in shape. Each major wine calls for its own traditionally shaped glass.

When pressed glass became popular, drinking glasses were produced in hundreds of patterns. Some of the best-known ones include almond thumbprint, argus, blaze, bull's-eye, frosted leaf, gothic, honeycomb, horn of plenty, inverted fern, pineapple, ribbed bellflower, ribbed grape, and waffle.

Some idea of the number of tumblers and goblets produced in this country can be given by examining the output of a single company which specialized in these pieces: A. J. Beatty of Steubenville, Ohio. After acquiring an established factory, Beatty razed the old furnaces and built new ones large enough to accommodate his production capacity. The factory operated at full blast during the Civil War. Beatty employed 130 men regularly, and turned out an average of 36,000 glasses a day. He became the country's leading producer of glasses, shipping his wares to every port in the world, competing successfully with French, English, and German glass products.

111 *The form and decoration of all pressed-glass pieces start with the patternmaker's wooden mold. Opposite are a number of these wooden molds with their glass counterparts alongside. At the left of the bottom row is the plaster model made from the wooden mold for the inverted-fern sauce dish; in the center, the wooden and metal mold for the shell pattern. At the right is the three-part plaster model from which metal molds were cast for the inverted-fern egg cup. Photograph by Hugo Poisson, courtesy Sandwich Glass Museum, Sandwich, Massachusetts*
112 *Tumblers were produced in a great variety of designs and were blown, mold-blown, or pressed. This undecorated one with a rounded bottom is from the early 1800s*

47

◀ 111

113 *Wide-footed flip glass made by several different glassworks, early nineteenth century* 114 *Tumbler with fluted sides and beading* 115 *Blown-three-mold glass tumbler with varying rows of geometric designs, including swirls, fluting, and all-over diamond-diaper pattern* 116 *Six-sided small whisky glass, early nineteenth century* 117 *Tall-stemmed goblet of pressed glass* 118 *Heavy, footed tumbler, six-sided with arch design* 119 *Thin glass tumbler of expanded diamond-mold design, possibly the most popular early pattern, c. 1810–20* 120 *Stemmed wine goblet with two flanges at the stem*

117

118

119

120

49

Pitchers & Decanters

122

123

124

SOME OF THE MOST distinctive pitchers and creamers were South Jersey pieces. Generally, the South Jersey pitcher had a short neck in proportion to the body, or an applied foot of a short-stemmed form. There were several broad classifications of pitchers: globular body, tapering to a lightly flaring rim, with a stemmed circular foot; globular body with a short cylindrical neck and a tiny pinched lip, sometimes having a petaled foot or solid loop handle; cylindrical body, short shoulder and neck, with a slight flare at the rim (larger pitchers usually had a strap handle); slender barrel shape, sometimes called mug shape, with a pinched lip; and a graceful, tapering pear shape, approaching a globular body, but having a slightly longer neck and wider rim, sometimes folded, with a small or deep pinched lip. Most of these vessels were free blown. Decorative effects were achieved by shaping or coloring, or by the application of a layer of glass tooled into a heavy swirl—swagged, ribbed, or threaded—or formed into the lily pad. Other forms of ornamentation, such as prunts, quilling, and rigaree, were also used. In later pieces combinations of colors were applied in swirls, loops, or striations. No matter how graceful the shape and decorative treatment, the thickness of the glass invested the fragile objects with a quality of sturdiness.

The early pitchers in the Stiegel tradition embrace a wide variety of types and decorative techniques. The shapes were more sophisticated and expertly formed than were the South Jersey types and faithfully followed English and Continental prototypes. Decoration varies: wheel cut, shallow stylized engraving, enameling, and expanded pattern-molded designs, such as paneling, ribbing, fluting, and variations of the Venetian diamond.

Cruets and castor bottles, small variants of

121 *Display of blown-three-mold glass, designed in the main by Deming Jarvis (1790–1869) at the Sandwich glassworks. The pitcher on the top shelf at left shows the diamond sunburst alternating with diamond diapering in the wide band; the creamer at the right is light gray-blue with fluted sides. On second shelf, third from left, pint chain with heart-design decanter, blown hollow stopper; at right, deep sapphire blue decanter in shell and ribbing pattern with matching stopper. On third shelf at right, carafe with peacock eye and two bands around neck. On fourth shelf at left, sapphire blue toilet or vinegar bottle in vertical ribbing with band at top. On bottom shelf, from left: quart decanter in arch-and-fern pattern with snake medallion and inscription* RUM; *quart pitcher in pattern mold; quart decanter, double-patterned over diamond-sunburst pattern, with vertical ribbing and matching stopper; quart decanter in diamond-sunburst alternating with diamond-diaper band and famous Sandwich acorn stopper, the rarest of stoppers* 122 *Pitcher with large bird's-eye bowl, straight narrow neck, and ribbed handle* 123 *Ribbed or fluted cruet with matching stopper* 124 *Wine carafe with large stopper in brilliant flint with overlay. Center area of bowl decorated with grape-and-vine motif*

51

125

126

127

128

129

the pitcher form which held vinegar, oil, or other condiments, were made in both the Stiegel and the South Jersey types. They are lipped bottles which have either metal tops or glass stoppers and are produced with or without handles. When offered in a set, they were supplied in a cruet or castor frame. They were in general use from about 1750 to the early twentieth century.

The decanter is a vessel which rests on a flat base without footing; the lower portion is usually globular in shape, tapering to a narrow lipped opening. The method of transition from the lower liquid-holding section to the upper narrow neck lends itself to varied interpretation, as does the technique of manufacture and

125 *Ruby cut-glass creamer with diamond-patterned bowl and pronounced scalloped rim, c. 1870–80* **126** *Cream pitcher of flint glass with Baroque pattern, c. 1825–40* **127** *Hand-blown water pitcher of mottled glass, ribbed, 1850* **128** *Hand-blown pitcher with loopings of opaque white, c. 1825–50* **129** *Hobnail pitcher with ribbed handle, made by Boston and New England Glass Company* **130** *Straight-sided bowl pitcher of Cambridge glass, 1883*

130

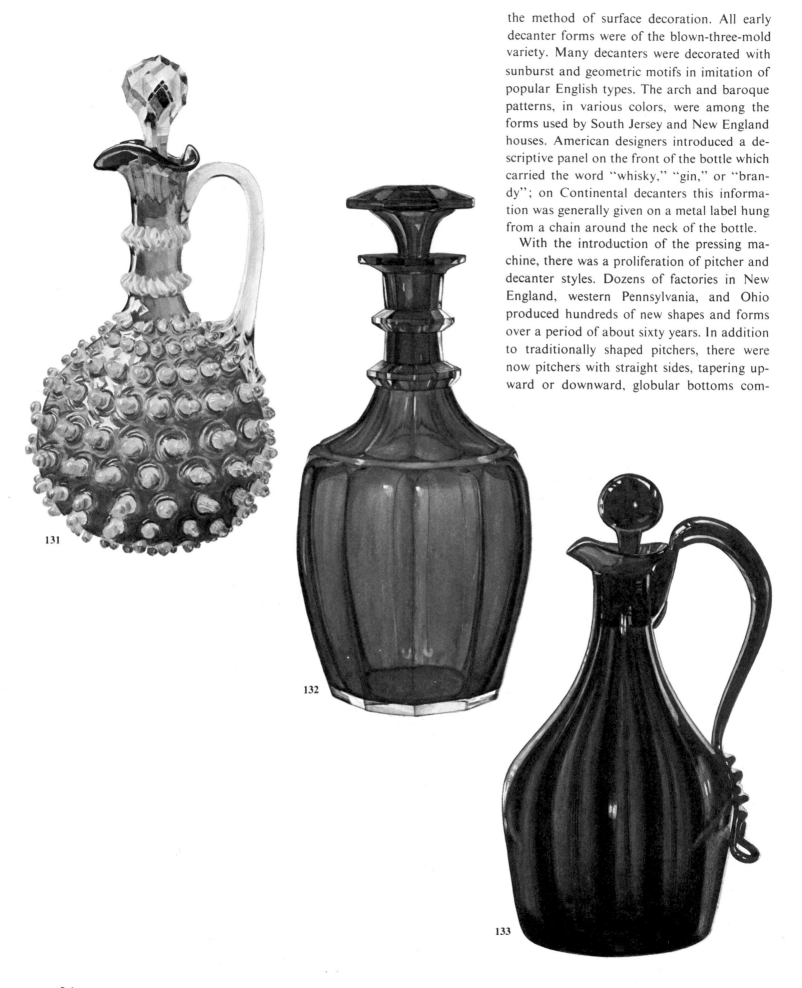

the method of surface decoration. All early decanter forms were of the blown-three-mold variety. Many decanters were decorated with sunburst and geometric motifs in imitation of popular English types. The arch and baroque patterns, in various colors, were among the forms used by South Jersey and New England houses. American designers introduced a descriptive panel on the front of the bottle which carried the word "whisky," "gin," or "brandy"; on Continental decanters this information was generally given on a metal label hung from a chain around the neck of the bottle.

With the introduction of the pressing machine, there was a proliferation of pitcher and decanter styles. Dozens of factories in New England, western Pennsylvania, and Ohio produced hundreds of new shapes and forms over a period of about sixty years. In addition to traditionally shaped pitchers, there were now pitchers with straight sides, tapering upward or downward, globular bottoms combined with straight necks, footed and stemmed base combinations, legged bases, and a variety of handles with curved, straight, and broken members. As the Victorian age advanced, the tendency was to heavy ornamentation of entire surfaces. Any attempt to categorize the different decorative treatments reads like a history of ornament. Geometric cuts, ribs, flutes, and cross-hatching into diamond and lozenge patterns follow the traditional cut-glass decoration of the Anglo-Irish school. Naturalistic motifs abound, including leaf, flower, bird, and animal forms in a variety of combinations. Panels enclosing Classical figures and cameos were used in contrast with architectonic arrangements, columns, and flutings of many styles. With the public's seemingly endless appetite for more and more decoration, and the patternmakers' efforts to keep up with the entreaties of their sales departments, the elegance and restraint which had characterized earlier pitchers and decanters was lost.

136

135

134

131 *Hobnail pressed-glass vinegar cruet with faceted stopper and blown handle. Made in West Virginia, c. 1875* **132** *Hand-blown carafe with ten side panels. Made in Cambridge, Massachusetts, c. 1840* **133** *Cruet of flint glass blown in dip mold and expanded in pattern of vertical fluting. Made in Pittsburgh, 1800–1825* **134** *Hand-blown gemel bottle for vinegar and oil with silver inlay decoration. Made in New Orleans, 1820* **135** *Cruet of pigeon-blood pressed glass with vertical ribbing. Made in Pittsburgh, c. 1830* **136** *Molasses or syrup jar of striped glass with raised, molded design and silver-plated copper top, c. 1850*

Candy Jars, Compotes & Cup Plates

138

PRESSED GLASSWARE was found to be ideal for flat or shallow pieces. Service plates, tea plates, cup plates, compotes, trays, spoon and celery holders, candy jars, salts, and covered dishes for butter, cake, and sugar were produced in great numbers. Most of these articles were pressed in clear glass, although a variety of colors, including amethyst, sapphire, green, ruby, amber, canary, and citron, were also used. Exciting designs were created by contrasting large motifs like leaves, palmettes, and bull's-eyes with cross-hatched, beaded, or diamond-cut areas, in imitation of the more expensive cut glass. Characteristic design motifs included acanthus leaves, scrolls, palmettes, peacock feathers, hearts, sunbursts, tulips, fleur-de-lys, roses, thistles, daisies, lyres, cornucopias with fields of diamond point, and strawberry diamonds.

Cup plates became the largest single tableware item produced by the various factories, although they had only an incidental use: to hold a tea cup. It is difficult to determine why the simple little cup plate should have become so popular. Perhaps this popularity stemmed from the widely accepted nineteenth-century custom of sipping tea or coffee from the saucer, or perhaps it was another manifestation of the collector's mania. Whatever the reason, dozens of houses vied with one another in issuing hundreds of new patterns to meet the demands of the market. The design of cup plates falls into three categories: conventional designs, both geometric and naturalistic; historical; and semihistorical and pictorial. Among the subjects depicted on the flat circular center of the cup plate are portraits, especially of George Washington; eagles in many forms; log cabins; various commemorative subjects, such as the Bunker Hill Monument, the *Constitution*, and the *Clermont*; railroads, stagecoaches, plows, and all types of symbols and figures.

Designs produced by a factory which were especially successful with the public, such as log-cabin and Henry Clay cup plates, were immediately copied by scores of other factories. Sometimes these imitations were exact replicas of the originals; sometimes variations were introduced. Molds were occasionally exchanged between houses on a friendly basis.

Production of other items of tableware, particularly jars, bowls, compotes, and butter and cake dishes, increased with the public's desire for new patterns to accompany each new season. The changing styles in design motifs which occur throughout the field of pressed glassware can be traced in the patterns of these articles. In the late 1830s and early '40s, complicated designs appeared, imitating popular patterns in cut glass. Among these are New England pineapple, horn of plenty, comet, four petal, and Sandwich star. In the 1850s many patterns were characterized by vertical ribbing. Included in this group are ribbed grape, ivy, ribbed acorn, fine rib, ribbed

137 *A selection of lacy pressed glass dating from about 1825 to 1850, and pressed pattern glass, about 1840–70. Most of the pieces were produced at the Boston and Sandwich Glass Company and the New England Glass Company. Mechanical pressing of glass, an American invention of about 1825, gave great impetus to glass production and was readily adopted in England and Europe. Photograph courtesy Corning Museum of Glass, Corning, New York*
138 *Cobalt glass sugar bowl designed by Stiegel. Made in Manheim, Pennsylvania, c. 1770*

139

140

141

142

143

palm, inverted fern, southern ivy, and bell-flower. The bellflower pattern is to be found in the greatest number of articles with ribbed designs. By the 1860s and '70s, at the height of the Victorian Age, elaborate designs done in high relief and displaying naturalistic motifs were popular.

139 *Butter dish and cover of red enamel over clear pressed glass. Made in Pittsburgh, c. 1890* **140** *Sapphire blue sugar bowl with octagonal side panels, turned up scalloped rim, and paneled dome with acorn finial. Made in Pittsburgh, c. 1850*
141 *Hand-blown sugar bowl with cover of clear flint glass and loopings of rose and white. Clear glass knob, stem, and circular foot. Made in Cambridge, 1825–50*
142 *Lidded sugar bowl on stem and footing. Probably made in Sandwich, 1830*
143 *Deep blue glass sugar bowl with lid. Made in Pittsburgh, 1830* **144** *Covered butter dish in sawtooth pattern, c. 1855–60*

144

145 *Pressed-glass compote without lid. Pattern is a variant of the daisy-and-button design, c. 1890* 146 *Pressed-glass compote or fruit bowl with dewdrop design and stippled panels, c. 1875–80* 147 *Pressed-glass compote, c. 1880*
148 *Pressed-glass compote with paneled sides and stem and circular footing* 149 *Clear pressed-glass fruit bowl on stem with variant of bull's-eye design* 150 *Compote with sultan, or curtain, pattern. Made in Pittsburgh, 1866* 151 *Deep pressed-glass bowl on stem. Fluted sides with scalloped base and rim* 152 *Pressed-glass bowl with bull's-eye pattern and circular footed base. Photographs from the Index of American Design*

149

150

151

152

153

154

153 *Clear pressed-glass cup plate with lyre design, c. 1830–40* **154** *Octagonal plate, c. 1830. Cusped medallion with eagle bordered by stars in circles* **155** *Clear pressed-glass cup plate with hearts and palmettes, c. 1831* **156** *Opalescent pressed-glass cup plate with heart motif in outer rim, c. 1835–50* **157** *Clear cup plate, c. 1830. Large American eagle encircled by stars, border, and scalloped rim* **158** *Decorative octagonal cup plate with the frigate* Constitution *in center, c. 1830 All photographs courtesy Corning Museum of Glass, Corning, New York*

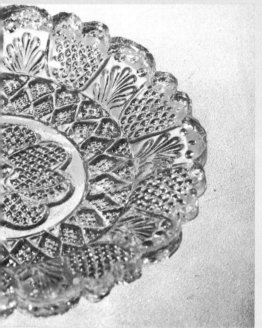

155

156

157

158

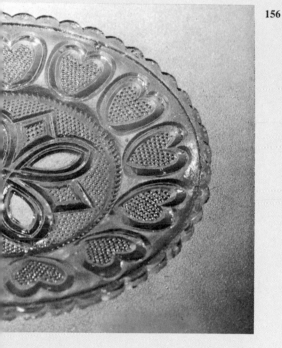

Bottles & Flasks for John Barleycorn

160

161

ONE WOULD HAVE TO search far and wide to find a single area in which greater inventiveness has been displayed than in the design of nineteenth-century bottles and flasks. The first product of organized glassmakers, bottles were made by about 95 percent of all companies in the industry. There were bottles for bitters, wine, rum, cider, and medicine; bottles for ink, cleaning fluids, kerosene, camphine, rattlesnake oil, bear's grease, and nostrums of all kinds. Gin, whisky, and cordials were bottled in flasks of all shapes and sizes, from ten-gallon carboys to half-ounce vials. There were squares, ovals, log cabins, fiddles, cornucopias, and calabashes produced in clear glass and in a wide variety of colors, including rose, blue, amethyst, aqua, purple, amber, pale and dark green, and even black. The design treatments were so varied that it has been said that American history can be traced through the subject matter on glass bottles.

The terms "flask" and "pocket bottle" were used interchangeably to describe the majority of bottle types: forms with flat or convex surfaces rising to a shoulder and narrow neck, oval or elliptical in cross section. Usually both sides of the flask or bottle were decorated, sometimes with names and inscriptions. Purely decorative designs were used as well as pictorial representations showing patriotic motifs, portraits of presidents, historical figures and heroes of the day, and social and political events. Sunbursts, urns, cornucopias, wreaths, sheaves of wheat, ears of corn, and geometric designs decorated one side or were secondary to pictorial themes on the reverse side.

By far the greatest variety of motifs included symbols of patriotic interest such as the eagle, the American flag, Columbia, and the stars and the shield. Over a hundred different flasks used the eagle as the central theme, sometimes as the only decoration, or on the reverse side of flasks featuring portraits of national heroes. The eagle was also paired with Columbia, the Masonic emblem, the American flag, a scroll and floral medallion, sunburst or cornucopia, or the railroad. The constant recurrence of the eagle motif, a symbol of strength and sovereignty, indicates the spirit of unity that marked the first half of the nineteenth century.

The most popular figure for portraits was George Washington. Busts of Washington appeared on more than sixty different types of flask, most of which were molded between 1820 and 1830. Many Washington flasks have the American eagle on the reverse side; others show a ship, a sheaf of wheat, the Baltimore Monument, or portraits of statesmen or generals.

159 *Figured flasks, some with pictorial and historical subjects, produced in various glass-houses throughout the United States, c. 1815–75. They are approximately half-pint, pint, and quart capacity. This type of flask is a peculiarly American phenomenon in glass; only a few pictorial flasks were produced in Europe. Photograph courtesy Corning Museum of Glass, Corning, New York* 160 *Two views of rare eagle flask. On the front, the American eagle with head to the left, shield on breast. On the reverse, eagle in flight carrying a serpent in its beak* 161 *Bitters bottle in the form of an Indian squaw*

162

163

164

65

167

168

166

162 *Stiegel-type perfume bottle, about half-pint size, with free-blown diamond-daisy design* **163** *Blown-three-mold decanter with diamond-sunburst design and swirled fluting. Made by Mt. Vernon Glass Company, c. 1820–35* **164** *Stiegel perfume bottle with honey comb pattern and ribbed neck, fluting in lower half, c. 1770* **165, 166** *Obverse and reverse sides of pint-size flask feature large urn with five vertical bars and cornucopia filled with produce* **167** *Stiegel-type pattern-molded flint toilet bottle with broken swirl fluting, late eighteenth century* **168** *Pint flask with large elliptical sunburst design and horizontally corrugated edging, c. 1815* **169** *Scroll flask with elaborate decoration forming conventionalized acanthus leaves; diamond motif at center. Probably of Pittsburgh manufacture*

169

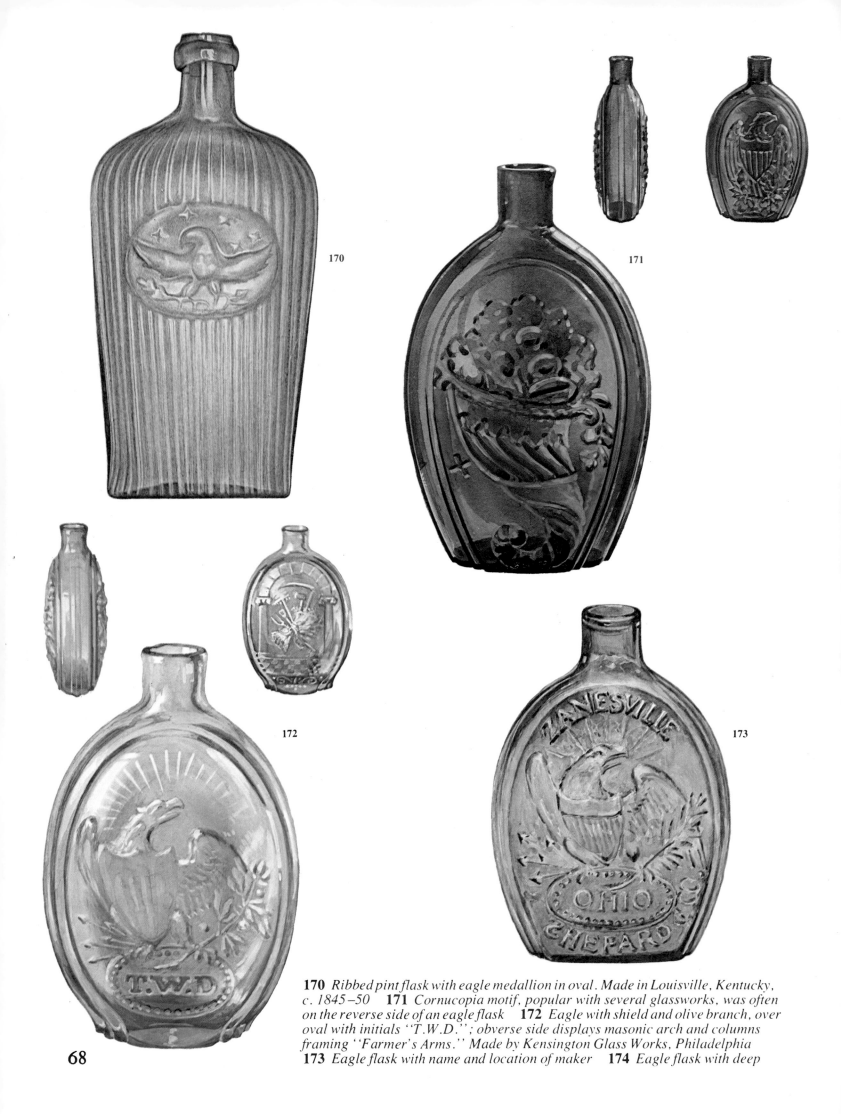

170

171

172

173

170 *Ribbed pint flask with eagle medallion in oval. Made in Louisville, Kentucky, c. 1845–50* **171** *Cornucopia motif, popular with several glassworks, was often on the reverse side of an eagle flask* **172** *Eagle with shield and olive branch, over oval with initials "T.W.D."; obverse side displays masonic arch and columns framing "Farmer's Arms." Made by Kensington Glass Works, Philadelphia* **173** *Eagle flask with name and location of maker* **174** *Eagle flask with deep*

*modeling, giving high relief to details. Made by Lancaster Glass Works,
c. 1850–60* **175** *Eagle flask with the word "Liberty." Made in Connect-
icut* **176** *Masonic flask with agricultural implements in archway.
Made by Kensington Glass Works, Philadelphia* **177** *Flask featuring General
Zachary Taylor and George Washington on opposite sides. Made by Bridgeton
Glass Works, New Jersey*

69

Please  Be Seated

179

THE CHAIR, man's simple yet ingenious "machine for comfort," has for over three thousand years been a sign of his civilization, an accepted symbol of status, an indicator of social change, and a yardstick of technological progress. From the *klismos* of ancient Greece, at once graceful and decorative yet strictly functional, to the inflatable plastic forms of the contemporary scene or the form-fitting contour shapes designed for the astronauts, the chair's main purpose has been to rest man's body and relax his system.

From the beginning of the New England settlement there were the Carver chairs with turned members, spindle-backs and also slat-backs, named for John Carver, who was the Colony's first Governor. The earliest examples of this chair were very clumsy, but over the years it was gradually refined. The Brewster chair is generally similar but it is a trifle more ornamental in its many turnings, which number about forty spindles per chair, sometimes even more.

By the last decade of the seventeenth century, joiners and furniture makers in small towns as well as larger cities had expanded their trade into a flourishing industry. While English influences predominated, the Colonial craftsmen were already exhibiting an independence of their own by simplifying forms and eliminating extra embellishments. Banister-back chairs with four or five vertical slats topped by a cresting between stiles were an outgrowth of the more formal William and Mary cane-backed chair. Two flat pieces, temporarily fastened together, were turned on a lathe and then separated; the resulting spindles matched and had flat surfaces. This is just one small example of the ingenuity introduced by native chairmakers within the framework of existing styles imported from abroad.

A most common and popular type of chair is the slat-back that evolved from the heavier form of Puritan chair with turned uprights and three horizontal slats across the back, which was made from 1670 to 1700. Throughout the eighteenth century the slat-back prevailed, with variants in two broad classes: the New England type and that of Pennsylvania. The New England chairs, like their Puritan precursors, are constructed with slats whose lower edges are straight and whose upper edges are curved. Their uprights are turned with rings and beads corresponding to the spaces between slats. In the Pennsylvania version the slats, as many as six compared to the limit of four in the New England type, are curved, with pronounced arched upswings on both top and bottom edges. Front stretchers show ball or sausage turning, side stretchers are plain. Both types of slat-back chairs use rush seats. Both were made with and without arms, and also in miniature form as a child's chair; their uprights are most frequently of maple or birch, with slats and stretcher parts of oak, ash, beech, or hickory.

The short period of Queen Anne's reign

178 *Parlor of the Governor's Palace, Williamsburg, Virginia. The artistry of master cabinetmakers is evident in the upholstered chairs as well as in the other mid-eighteenth-century fine furnishings and architectural detailing of fireplace and mantel. Photograph courtesy Colonial Williamsburg* **179** *Mahogany side chair with eagle splat. Attributed to Duncan Phyfe, c. 1815*

180

181

182

(1702–14) was important in furniture design in England and in the Colonies. In America the style identified as Queen Anne was popular from 1720 to 1750, although its influence lingered on until the close of the century. In the early 1700s the many alien strains that had crept into English designs in the previous generations were more fully assimilated. The Baroque details of Continental origin popular in the reigns of Charles II, James II, and William and Mary, which incorporated intricate patterns, reverse scrolls, and curves, were replaced by a more sober style in keeping with the English dislike for ornamental extravagance. Characteristic of the Queen Anne style was a blending of form and function and the dominance of the curve typified by the graceful, undulating sweep of the cabriole legs on chairs, tables, and other supports. Popular acceptance of the style was widespread in the cities and smaller towns of the main river valleys, where it was identified not only by the curve of the legs but by serpentine stretchers, rounded splats, undulating crests for chair tops, and lower aprons gracefully arched in cyma-curvate shapes.

72

183

184

It has been said that many of the sophisticated amenities of home comfort and utility had their origins in the Queen Anne period. Not only chairs but many other articles designed for comfort and convenience in the home, such as tea, gaming, and dressing tables, mirrors, and frames came into being or were perfected at this time. Earlier Puritan stiffness typified by the hard-seated wainscot chair now

180 *Chair in the Queen Anne style, featuring curved stiles and splat formed by parallel curves and cabriole legs with carved shells at the knees, c. 1730. The claw-and-ball feet are found on many of the later Queen Anne chairs* **181** *Chippendale-style side chair with ornamental pierced splat, carved shells, and claw-and-ball feet, c. 1760–80* **182** *Chair in the Queen Anne style, with four turned stretchers and vase-shaped splat, c. 1730* **183** *Chippendale-style side chair, distinguished by carved cresting and splat* **184** *Armchair in the early Chippendale style with club feet; vase-shaped splat and carved shells at top of the crest and on chair front, c. 1760* **185** *Side chair in the American Directoire style with curved top rail and carved crosspiece, c. 1810–25*

185

186

melted into grace and classic symmetry as carving gave way to beautifully proportioned flat or contoured surfaces, form-fitting for bodily comfort.

The characteristics of Chippendale-type chairs, while not adhering to any rigidly recognizable formula, have certain features in common. Top rails usually follow the "cupid's bow" curvature, with the two ends or "ears" curved upward. Another top rail variant, not as common as the cupid's bow, carries three curves in a downward design. The back splats are most often pierced, though the solid splat outlined with scrolls occurs in many instances. The open or pierced splats present a great variety of designs, many elaborately formed; some are leaf-carved or interwoven, others carry Gothic details or a lozenge motif. Chippendale's twenty plates of chair styles, displaying over sixty designs, were copied with fidelity,

188

187

189

186 *New England wing chair, upholstered with block-printed cotton of East Indian floral design. Turned bulbous stretchers, a survival from the seventeenth century, and boldly carved Spanish feet on forelegs, c. 1725* **187** *Sheraton-style armchair with rectangular back, top rail raised and reeded, and three slender and graceful pierced banisters, c. 1800–1810* **188** *Hepplewhite-style chair, with high arched back and delicately carved, pierced splat, c. 1785–1800* **189** *Sheraton-style "drawing-book chair," so-called because it derives from Sheraton's design manual. Open rectangular back with pierced vase and festoons, surmounted by Prince of Wales feathers, c. 1795–1810*

or served as the basis for variations devised by the Colonial chairmakers.

The nomenclature of this era presents a confusing array of terms which does little to clarify the many currents and crosscurrents for the layman. The French Empire style, initiated with Napoleon's ascendancy in 1804, found its counterpart in the American Empire style. This style reflects the continuing interest in Classical motifs and forms, which was expressed in designs intended actually to reproduce ancient furniture models. The most notable American furniture maker of the Classic Revival period was Duncan Phyfe, and the designs produced by him and his contemporaries were many and varied.

190

191

192

193

190–195, 196 *The technique of bronze stenciling Hitchcock-type chairs and Boston rockers was in vogue from 1820 to 1850, although the practice continued beyond this period. The stencil was cut from stiff paper, oiled cardboard, or thin sheet metal; in manufacturing, metal was preferred for durability in mass production. The color was applied through the apertures of the stencil with a stubby brush or dauber. Fruits and flowers, liberally enhanced by leaf forms, were dominant motifs* **194** *"Fancy chairs" such as this one were advertised by the "chair manufactories" located in the leading cities of the eastern seaboard. Lambert Hitchcock of Barkhamsted, Connecticut, was the most important maker*

194

Painted & Stenciled

IN THE FIRST QUARTER of the nineteenth century "fancy chairs" became popular. By 1825 every town of any size had a woodworking shop whose sign usually read: "Fancy and Windsor Chairmaker." Leading cities along the coast had many such shops. One of the men who gave impetus to the movement was Lambert Hitchcock of Connecticut.

Hitchcock began by manufacturing chair parts and shipping the unassembled backs, seats, slats, and stretchers, which were assembled on arrival. Since there was no artisan group in the South to supply the furniture needs of the average person, these chairs found a ready market in Charleston, South Carolina, and other growing southern coastal cities. Hitchcock's simple yet unique procedure was adopted by manufacturers of inexpensive furniture. (The finished chair, painted and decorated, sold for a dollar and a half.)

After a few years, Hitchcock abandoned this method and began to sell the assembled chairs. He was the first to mass-produce these chairs. The different parts were combined on an assembly-line, following the philosophy of enterprising Connecticut clock manufacturers: "Why make one or two when we can turn them out by the hundreds, and then paint and decorate them just as clock dials and tablets are painted." Hitchcock employed over a hundred hands in his factory, including many women and children whom he trained in the art of decorating the painted surfaces. The industry became so important that the name of the town was changed from Barkhamsted to Hitchcocksville. The term "Hitchcock chair," as usually employed, was generic rather than specific. It was applied to a wide range of chairs produced roughly between 1825 and 1830 with stencil-decorated surfaces, in gold or other colors.

Stenciling, an ancient handcraft, was a short cut to painting surfaces by hand. Much Early American decoration used stenciled patterns on walls and floors in floral or festoon motifs,

195

196

197 *Ladder-back Hitchcock armchair of curly maple with crude and uncertain painted decoration, c. 1820* **198** *Hand-painted chair with decoration imitating stencil motifs* **199** *Curved top rail and turned spindles and legs add decorative interest to Hitchcock-type chair, c. 1840* **200** *Hitchcock chair has slightly arched concave top rail, turned only at the ends. Across the middle of the open back are a concave wide slat and a narrower one; usually only the wide one is decorated. Rush seat is protected by a split turning at the front. Made chiefly of maple and copied in a number of shops, c. 1820–50* **201** *Cane-seated Hitchcock chair with wide back slat displaying graceful fruit basket with leaf forms. Flattened portions of back uprights decorated. Turned forelegs splayed with gilding on beading throughout* **202** *All-wooden painted chair, with concave top rail and slat prominent areas of decoration*

200

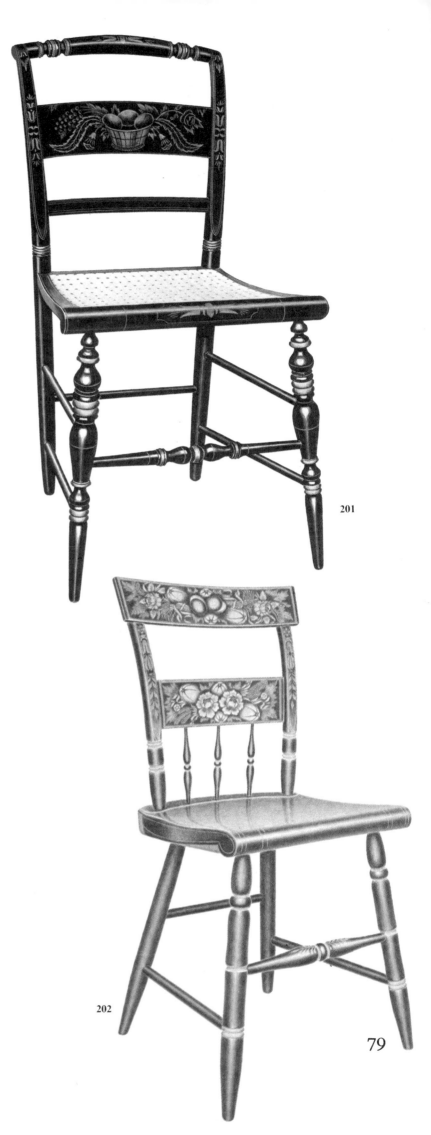

201

and in geometric shapes as borders or all-over diapers. Stenciled ornamentation was widely used on wallpaper, bandboxes, decorated coverlets, trays, and toleware, and on clock dials and the glass panels which were inserted in shelf clocks and banjo clocks, Stenciled forms in countless arrangements were used in creating the charming theorem paintings composed of fruits, flowers, leaves, and baskets.

The typical Hitchcock chair combined the best features of the Sheraton and French Directoire styles. It was of maple. It had a slightly arched top rail, either turned or shaped, leaving a flat middle section for the application of a stenciled design. Front legs were turned, with shallow ring or bead turnings, and tapered slightly to terminate in small ball feet.

The painted fancy chairs of Hitchcock and his contemporaries were widely used in pleasure palaces, hotel lobbies, theater boxes, ice-cream parlors, and canal and river steamers. ("Cleopatra's Barge" was another name by which these fancy chairs were known.)

202

203

204

The World of Windsors

THE ORIGIN of the Windsor chair has been traced to the English countryside at the time of George II, through a charming anecdote. Tradition says the king sought refuge during a fierce storm in a peasant's cottage near Windsor Castle. He sat in a crudely fashioned chair, made of upright spindles, and remarked on the rare comfort and utter simplicity of its design. The chair impressed him so much that he had it copied by his cabinetmaker. News of this little episode spread, and with it the vogue for the chair, which was marketed from Windsor. Within a few years the Windsor chair reached American shores, where it was readily adopted, its popularity lasting from about 1725 to 1860. Although the earlier date is commonly mentioned, the first known documentation points to Governor Patrick Gordon of Pennsylvania, who died in 1736 and whose inventory listed five Windsor chairs. The same year, Hannah Hodge, a Philadelphia widow, included Windsor chairs among her household effects.

American Windsor chairs have been made in a great number of styles. For purposes of identification, six basic types may be described: low back, comb back, hoop back, New England arm, fan back, and loop back. All types have certain similar characteristics, and the most noticeable are the slender, round, upright spokes or spindles, turned and generally tapering upward. The spindles vary in number but present a graceful outline filled with evenly spaced thin parallel lines. On some types, the spindles at the seat are closer together and fan out as they reach the top rails or loops. The chair backs are slanted backward and are curved laterally to accommodate the back. The arms of the armchair slant outward. As a rule, the spindles taper or bulge slightly on finer examples; in some instances, a bamboo effect is simulated. The seats were made of a single plank, hollowed out in the fashion known as saddle seat.

Windsor chairs, unlike the other furniture products, were never made of walnut, cherry, or mahogany. They were usually fabricated from several kinds of wood: the hoop or bow of the back from hickory; the spindles and arms from hickory or ash; the legs from oak, hickory, or maple; and the seats from pine, whitewood, or beech. To camouflage this assortment of woods, the chairs, originally intended for garden, tavern, or outdoor use, were painted in a variety of colors. Green,

203 *Boston rocker with the grace and sturdiness characteristic of Windsor chairs: the tapered back spindles, scrolled top rail, and shaped seat combine to form a most efficient piece of household furniture. Made by Hitchcock, Alford and Company, c. 1832–40* **204** *Popular hoop-back Windsor, also called "bow-back," first produced by New England makers as a side chair. Raked legs and front and side stretchers, c. 1750–1800*

205 *Low-backed firehouse Windsor with back extension, eight turned spindles, and U-shaped continuous arm ending in scrolls, c. 1840–65* **206** *Low-backed Windsor writing chair with convenient storage drawer. Continuous arm terminates in and is supported by turned spindles; extreme splay of legs produces extra rigidity* **207** *Hoop-back Windsor with intersecting semicircular rail that forms arm ends, supported by turned spindles, c. 1750–1800* **208** *Comb-back Windsor with thick horizontal rail terminating in scrolls and arm supports of English derivation. Spindles extend upward to support a gracefully shaped comb, c. 1740–80* **209** *Rod-back Windsor with turned spindles and legs; sloping back is supported by uprights with knob finials joined by top rail, c. 1800–1830* **210** *Comb-back Windsor writing chair with six thin spindles forming comb support. Turned legs joined by H-stretcher support seat of unusual front design*

205

207

206

either dark green or apple green, seems to have been the favorite color at first. Then a variety of colors including black, Indian red, yellow, gray, brown, blue, and at times a touch of gold were used.

Wallace Nutting, a noted American furniture expert, admirably sums up the case for Windsors: "The merit and special charm of the Windsor chair are so often overlooked or unknown that we wish here, with almost brutal emphasis, to say that lightness was the chief purpose of the Windsor, to follow the heavy late-Gothic furniture which a woman could not move without a struggle. Hence an American Windsor means a pine seat if it means anything good. Also delicate lines to secure lightness throughout. This includes strongly bulbous legs and a light back. Such chairs well made were durable because they were elastic and bore falls without breaking. In a good Windsor, lightness, strength, grace, durability and quaintness are all found in an irresistible blend."

208

209

210

Joiner &
Decorator
Join Hands

Toward the closing years of the seventeenth century, the art of japanning was introduced into this country from England, where it had caught the fancy of many cabinetmakers. The increasing British trade with the Orient had resulted in the importation of assorted goods from China, Japan, India, and Indochina. In Holland, an influx of Huguenot refugees learned the art, and the mania for everything Oriental was further stimulated and brought from Holland by William and Mary. An important volume written in 1688 by John Stalker and George Parker called A Treatise of Japanning fanned a raging controversy between the Classicists, on the one hand, and the proponents of Orientalism. The English furniture makers and their followers on Colonial shores plunged into an orgy of Oriental fantasies, covering surfaces of cabinets and highboys with chinoiserie that evoked a colorful realm of costumed figures, pagodas, toriis, temples and gardens, birds and beasts. The skillful practitioners of the art of japanning produced raised designs, built up with chalk compounds for relief.

211

Surfaces were highly polished, sized, and metal leaf was then affixed. "Lay on your gold," the Treatise advised, "if your work be sufficiently moist, you'll perceive how lovingly the gold will embrace it, hugging, and clinging to it...."

Colonial japanners used maple as a ground for their principal surfaces and pine for less important areas. After building up, polishing, and painting, several coats of varnish were applied to give permanence and luster to their painted efforts.

For their source material, the decorators and japanners turned to imported goods—principally the Oriental porcelains and Delft pottery, using motifs from the Far East and Indian calicoes. Various pattern books published by the leading British cabinetmakers contained plates of value as exemplars. In Chippendale's The Gentleman & Cabinet Maker's Director *many Oriental motifs are shown, particularly on the fire screens, tea chests, chimney pieces, and picture frames.*

212

213

211 *Painted chest of drawers ornamented with long, graceful stems, buds, blossoms, and stylized foliage is typical of a style that developed about 1700 in the area of Guilford, Connecticut. Tudor and Dutch design sources supplied the inspiration* **212** *Five-drawer highboy in the Queen Anne style with flat top, slender cabriole legs, and triple-arch base, c. 1720–50* **213** *Painted highboy in the William and Mary style with six trumpet legs, well-designed stretcher, and triple-arch skirt. Each drawer displays a playful* chinoiserie *composition. All side panels and lower skirt are painted, c. 1700–1710*

214

215

216

214 *Painted chest with wide upper panel enclosing desk compartments. Lower frame has double inverted cup legs, scalloped stretcher on ball or bun feet. Three front panels display related compositions in floral designs* 215 *The decorator utilized the three drawer-faces as an entire façade starting at the bottom and building upward with curving scrolls and tulip forms. Introduction of bird forms adds life and gaiety. Made in Guilford, c. 1710* 216 *Painted chest rendered in more vigorous strokes than usual. Drawer panels look similar, but there are minor variations* 217 *Guilford chest of pine and whitewood. Decoration shows playful originality. Introduction of faces on upper drawers is an unusual conceit. The flower-pot motif in the center, derived from Moravian sources, often appears in peasant art forms, particularly in Pennsylvania German decoration. Thistle blossom surmounted by a crown, rose, and fleur-de-lys are combined in a distinctively American way. End panel shows a boldly done tulip stem and opened blossom, c. 1690–1700*

217

87

218

219

220

Small Chests & Desk Boxes

221

218 *Painted Guilford chest with finely conceived decorative composition balanced on central stem. Branching out and upward, wavy scrolls show a strong calligraphic feeling with tulip and leaf forms highly conventionalized* 219 *Small chest with overhanging molding shows strong influence of printed wallpaper designs used extensively on bandboxes. Nineteenth century* 220 *Painted chest with molding grip under lid at the ends. Design in a series of borders; inner panel is handled ineptly; scrolls lack grace and flowing lines* 221 *End panel of 218. Totally linear treatment of naturalistic scroll forms displays originality. Similar to front panel, with variations* 222 *Gumwood bandbox with arched top hinged on leather straps and metal fastener. Box is covered in block-print paper, with hand-painted flowers* 223 *Small chest, about twenty inches long, with gadroon beaded molding top and bottom and skirt of scallop design. Tulip forms appear in original compositions: arboreal arrangement on each side and a ringlet at the center*

222

223

224

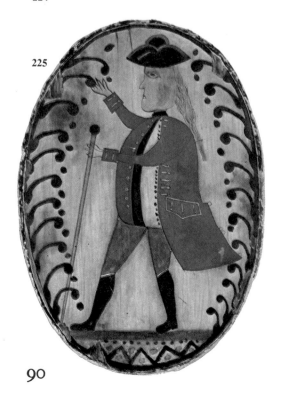

225

224 *The traditional Pennsylvania German style of decoration is much in evidence in this* Fraktur *room, so called because of the many baptismal certificates, house blessings, and framed sentiments written in Fraktur calligraphy. Typical also in this Berks County room are the two hand-painted dower chests at the rear. Second half of the eighteenth century. Photograph courtesy the Henry Francis du Pont Winterthur Museum, Winterthur, Delaware* **225** *Of the same period is this painted splint box, showing a man in a red coat with cane and tricorn hat and suggesting the festive occasion when this type of box was given* **226** *In many dower chests the architectonic division of space into panels effectively separated decorative elements. This one, made in 1787*

Decorated for Dowry

226

THE DOWER CHEST was a traditional part of every maiden's world; she began to fill it with linens and laces the moment she learned to sew. When she stitched her first sampler or embroidered her first linens, these were carefully stored in the chest until she was married. Dower chests were the first hope chests designed to serve both a utilitarian and a romantic function and great care went into their construction and decoration. They were generally three to four feet long and were placed in either the parlor or the bedroom. Some chests contained a built-in drawer or two, but this was not typical. To raise the chest off the floor and give it a more convenient height, various supports were used—the shoe or trestle foot, the ball foot, the ogee bracket, or ordinary bracket foot could be placed at the four bottom corners. All of these could easily be constructed from flat stock with a scroll or fret saw.

The woods most used for dower chests were pine, poplar, and walnut. The large expanse of the front and top surface of each chest invited the hand of the decorator, and at the same time a painted surface made the soft wood more durable. The farmer-carpenter, however, rarely attempted to decorate the chest himself, but preferred to wait for the itinerant decorator to make his accustomed rounds.

The painted chest of the Pennsylvania Germans varied little from eighteenth-century European peasant furniture which was made of inexpensive pine and decorated in color. The favorite background color was a soft blue; dark green, brown, and even black were used on occasion. On this background, the decorator deftly applied vases of flowers, stars, tulips, daisies, birds, angels, and unicorns. The front panel was often divided into an architectonic arrangement of two or three arched areas. The end panels utilized the same architectonic forms to extend the impact of the front facade. Often the decorator designed an interplay of motifs which extended from the front areas to the end panels.

In Pennsylvania, the tulip recalled the distant gardens of the Rhineland and was used extensively. The fuchsia and carnation were also popular. The heart, symbol of love, appeared in every medium employed by the folk artist. The huge star featured on the commodious barns in Lehigh and Montgomery counties appeared as a favorite motif in chest decoration. The unicorns on Berks County chests are a carry-over from medieval days, when they represented the guardians of maidenhood. The peacock, stitched on hand towels and painted on chests and toleware, was a respected weather prophet.

Most chests were painted to order; often the owner's name appeared with the date and year of execution. The lettering on many of these chests was often in the Germanic or *Fraktur* style, using Gothic letter forms. Chris-

227

228

227–232 *All marriage chests had lift lids; some featured bottom drawers, but otherwise their construction varied little. There is great ingenuity in their scheme of decoration, however, and diverse motifs are used. Double-arched panels, as in 228, 231, and 232, and triple arches, as in 229 and 230, assist in well-ordered design schemes in which urns, flowered arrangements, and unicorns appear*

92

229

230

tian Selzer (1749–1831) inscribed and painted some of the finest dower chests in the Pennsylvania region.

Another fine decorator was Heinrich Otto, who also had a printing shop in Ephrata. His favorite design motifs were parrots, peacocks, animated birds with twisted necks, floral forms, and leafy vines.

Except for a few names, the painter-decorators whose works are now on display in museum collections or in private homes remain anonymous.

231

232

233

234

Of Time & Timepieces

TIME HAS obliterated all trace of
the first clockmakers in America, with the possible exception
of one Thomas Nash, an early
settler in New Haven, whose estate inventory,
posted in 1658, listed a number of tools,
among them "one round plate for making
clocks." None of his work is known today, but
the fact that he owned clockmaking tools is a
strong indication that he was indeed a clockmaker. In those early days clocks were imported mainly from England and the Netherlands, and in such quantity that the potential
of the American market soon became apparent
to European clockmakers. Many of them
emigrated, settling in Boston, New York, New
Haven, Philadelphia, and other large towns,
and immediately started training apprentices,
since fine workmen were needed to make and
repair not only clocks but also precision
instruments.

A few extant clocks from the period of about
1715 are attributable to known makers, who
were among the earliest immigrants. These
men and their apprentices included such names

235

as Benjamin Chandlee (Maryland), Samuel
Bispham (Philadelphia), Benjamin and Timothy Cheney (East Hartford), Gawen Brown
(Boston), David Rittenhouse (Philadelphia),
Benjamin Bagnall (Boston), David Blaisdell
(Amesbury, Massachusetts), and Seth Youngs
(Hartford), as well as many others. During the
first half of the eighteenth century they produced some of the earliest classic, so-called
grandfather clocks. One of our finest examples
was made in 1791 by David Rittenhouse, who
was also a noted scientist, astronomer, mathematician, and a president of the American
Philosophical Society.

The early clockmakers were craftsmen in the
fullest sense of the word. Starting with rough
steel or brass blanks, they fashioned every
piece from start to finish. Brass was cast in
sand molds and then hardened by hammering.
Wheels were turned and teeth cut and shaped
with the crudest of tools. Working alone or
with an apprentice or two, the clockmaker
assembled the complete mechanism and built
the cabinet as well. If this did not keep him
sufficiently employed he turned to gold- and

233 *In the corner of the Kershner parlor, in Berks County, Pennsylvania, stands the stately
grandfather clock made by Jacob Graff, of Lebanon. It is in perfect harmony with its
surroundings—the recessed twenty-light window, the imposing armchair, a country version of
the Philadelphia Chippendale form, and the dower chest, only partly seen. The tall clock was
easily the most important single piece of household furniture, designed and built with care and
destined to become a treasured heirloom. Its dial is handsomely engraved and has the moon
attachment to foretell the rise and fall of the tides. The case echoes the curvature of the upper
dial, above which there is an arched opening and a hooded top with five finials. Photograph
courtesy the Henry Francis du Pont Winterthur Museum, Winterthur, Delaware*
234 *Hand-painted clock face with floral decorations in the spandrels and center circle*
235 *Tall clock with panels of crotch mahogany and satinwood inlays. Made by Simon Willard,
c. 1800*

236

237

96

238

239

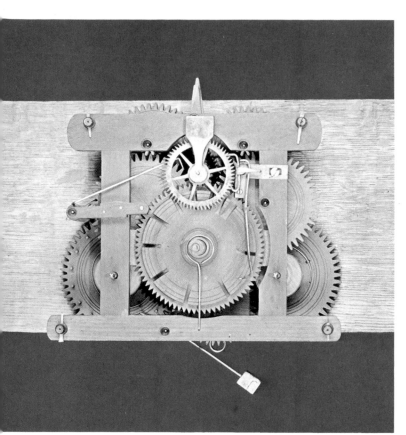

240

241

236 *Mantel clock with flat pediment, lathe-turned and stenciled pillars*   **237** *Eli Terry transitional clock, c. 1825–35*   **238** *Three-tier mantel clock with columns and eagle, c. 1835*   **239** *Clock of mahogany veneer; fine pilasters and carving*   **240, 241** *Detail showing wooden works and exterior of typical Seth Thomas clock. Photographs courtesy Shelburne Museum, Shelburne, Vermont*   **242** *Terry clock, crotched veneer, hand-stenciled, c. 1830*   **243** *Connecticut clock with scroll and colonnettes, c. 1830*

242

243

97

244

245

246

silversmithing, plate and tankard engraving, and the making of fine optical or ships' instruments. Some of the clockmakers are also known to have been locksmiths and gunsmiths.

In 1745 or thereabouts, the clockmaking industry, then centered in Connecticut, was affected by a revolutionary development—the replacement of brass works by hardwood works. This has been credited to Benjamin and Timothy Cheney of East Hartford. Many others in that vicinity began to use wood at that time, but the Cheney brothers were most successful and their influence seems to have been mainly responsible for the growth of the idea. The wooden works made by the Cheney brothers, Gideon Roberts, John Rich, and others were then installed in cases for grand-

father clocks. Although the mechanisms were crude, they were able to keep time accurately for thirty hours.

Two other Connecticut clockmakers deserving special mention are Thomas Harland, who settled in Norwich in 1773, and Daniel Burnap, who opened a shop in East Windsor about 1780. Both Harland and Burnap made a great number and variety of fine timepieces, using brass movements; some had musical attach-

ments. These men trained many apprentices. Most important among those taught by Burnap was Eli Terry, born in 1772, the son of a neighboring farmer. After completing his training, Terry opened a shop in Plymouth in 1793. His first clocks contained brass movement, but he soon experimented with hardwoods, using his previous experience at woodworking to perfect a method of making wooden movements in quantity.

244 *Tall clock by Benjamin Youngs, of Watervliet, New York. Severity of line suggests Shaker influence, 1806* **245** *Mahogany shelf clock called lyre clock, dominated by handsome pair of cyma scrolls, acanthus covered. Made by Aaron Willard and others, c. 1820* **246** *Tall clock with rounded hood, open fretwork, tall finials, decorated dial, and fine mahogany case. Possibly made by Ephraim Willard, c. 1780–95* **247** *Mahogany shelf clock, Gothic type. Decalcomania decorations on glass panels. Made by Birge and Fuller, c. 1845* **248** *Willard type of shelf clock with two distinct sections; also called Massachusetts shelf clock. Glass panels carry all-over decorations up to outer case, c. 1800–1820*

249 *Upper shelf, left to right: small jar covered in Albany slip, 1861 – 81; salt-glazed jar, applied "ear" handles, with rich cobalt blue decoration; earliest known piece of Norton stoneware, c. 1800; salt-glazed stoneware water cooler with cobalt blue flying-eagle motif, lined with Albany slip, c. 1861 – 81; miniature crock, with applied handles, decorated in cobalt. Lower shelf: small tan single-handled jug; two-handled jug probably for cider, marked "I. Judd, Jr. Bennington," c. 1830; earliest known piece of Bennington Pottery, made in 1798; two-handled jug with unusual eagle bas-relief and bands of incised decoration, made for A. Hathaway, 1838– 45; Albany slip bank made for Edward Norton. Photograph by Frank L. Forward, courtesy the Bennington Museum, Bennington, Vermont* **250** *Glazed stoneware wine jug with applied and incised decoration, made by Harris factory in Ohio, c. 1858* **251, 252** *Two bird motifs by early potters. These were blue slip designs from New York stoneware*

Jars & Jugs

250

Crocks & Churns

ALMOST ALL AMERICAN CERAMIC wares may be classified as pottery. Types are designated according to the clay used— red, yellow, gray, tan or white (common crockery). These various earthenwares and stonewares are opaque, whereas porcelain, or china, is translucent.

Common red clay, used for redware, is found along most of the eastern seaboard. It is easy to work, and as early as 1630 American potters were fashioning it into ordinary household plates, platters, pitchers, pots, jars, jugs, and crocks, as well as flowerpots, pipes, and roofing tiles. The potter dug his own clay— red clay lies close to the surface—and then, to eliminate impurities, ground it with a mill, or quern, a hand-operated device in which a millstone was turned inside of a larger stone. When larger amounts of clay were needed, the potter built a pug mill operated by horsepower. After the clay was cleaned, he then "wedged" or worked it further by hand, a process similar to the kneading of dough. When the wedged clay was ready to be turned, it was placed on the potter's wheel, a simple table with a rotating stand operated by foot. The potter then allowed his product to dry in the sun. This dried, unfired clay was called greenware. When there were enough pieces to fill the kiln and the fire was ready, the potter proceeded with the glazing and firing. Glazing helped

seal the extremely porous red-clay earthenware and lent a protective coating of brilliance and sparkle to an otherwise dull surface. The firing was done in a kiln by a wood fire that lasted from thirty to thirty-six hours, after which the kiln was allowed to cool before the pottery was removed.

The glaze, a compound of powdered red lead mixed with clay, fine sand, and water, produced an orange-red, dark-red, or brownish color. By adding manganese to the glaze, a brown or black resulted; similarly, by adding oxidized copper filings, a greenish color was produced. The charm of redware lies in the coloration and mottling of the glaze, and the brushings and dribblings of the green or brown as they flow down the surface. The earliest redware was decorated with slip, a liquid clay that was usually trailed on the surface of the unfired ware by being poured through a quill inserted in a clay slip cup.

Yellow earthenware was produced from a yellow or buff clay found in the regions of Ohio. This clay was primarily used for kitchen articles of Bennington flint enamel and Rockingham wares. Rockingham ware is dappled, streaked, or mottled to resemble a rich tortoise shell, with the application of a lustrous manganese brown glaze. From about the 1840s to 1900, it was used extensively in a great variety of household articles.

The custom of stamping the potter's name

251

252

253

254

255

256

257

258

on a piece became a common practice at the start of the nineteenth century. Nameplates were made from metal dies and impressed into the clay before firing. These were trademarks rather than a declaration of the potter's pride in his creation, for there was rarely much personal feeling about these common household objects which were destined for sale in the marketplace.

253–259 *Earthenware jugs and pitchers are not always dated, but the following information is well documented: figure 253, Philadelphia, c. 1865–70; 254, c. 1875–90; 255, 1868; 256, c. 1850; 257, Greensboro, Pennsylvania, 1797; 258, Waynesboro, Pennsylvania, c. 1830; 259, New York City, 1798. Most of these stoneware vessels are decorated with varying floral and foliated forms. The single-handled jug generally shows some ribbing at the neck, above which is a separate piece of decoration (as in 253, 257, and 258). The ovoid vessel form presents the greatest opportunity for decorative treatment at the wide portion of the belly. Some patterns employ symmetrical plant forms, while in others the forms move around the body of the vessel*

259

Stoneware jars, crocks, and jugs came in
varying sizes—some had a capacity as great as
thirty gallons—and shapes. Because they were
functional rather than ornamental, emphasis
was on simple, straightforward designs. Crocks
and preserve jars usually had straight sides, but
some bellied out at the middle of the body.
Jugs were single-handled vessels with a swell-
ing body and a small mouth for corking and
sealing. Although pottery usually kept to
these basic forms, the manner of decoration
provided an outlet for artistic self-expression.

260 *Jug decorated with vigorous floral
and leaf forms, 1850* **261** *Water jug with
pouring spout, decorated in the ''sgraffito''
manner of the Pennsylvania Germans,
1798* **262** *Stoneware wine keg with
outstanding relief treatment of the ribbing,
stars, and the especially competently
modeled eagle* **263** *Crock with freely
rendered eagle and shield, c. 1790–1820*
264 *Two-handled jug with incised and
slip-decorated birds and flowers. Probably
Pennsylvania German, 1844* **265** *Wine or
water jar with spigot hole. Plant and
flower forms in a charming, fluid design*
266 *Crock with lid and ''ears.'' The slight
neck and tapering body that swells at the base
create a pleasant shape to which decoration
has been tastefully applied*

260

261

262

263

264

265

266

267

267 *In the Harvest Room of the Dutton House, a modest cottage built in 1782, the dishes are placed on the broad-planked, pine dining table. From nearby Bennington, where Captain John Norton started making stoneware pottery in 1793, came pieces used for table service, including mottled ware plates, hound-handled pitchers, butter dishes, and the attractive centerpiece. Standing on the rear side bureau is a large Bennington octagonal water cooler and brown pitcher. The open dresser shelves display porcelain pitchers in various patterns and colors as well as a number of jugs and crocks. Photograph by Einmars J. Mengis, courtesy Shelburne Museum, Shelburne, Vermont* **268** *Small milk pitcher made at Bennington, c. 1850–60* **269** *Toby pitcher, a name derived from the popular English character Sir Toby Belch and designating a pitcher type first made by Staffordshire potters*

Rockingham & Bennington

268

AMERICAN ROCKINGHAM, THE ware for which Bennington, Vermont, became famous in the mid-nineteenth century, is English in origin and is named for the Marquis of Rockingham, whose works at Swinton produced a ware of a similar brownish color. The pottery itself is a cream-colored or yellow ware that is dipped or spattered with a brown glaze before firing. The mottled-brown glaze achieves an overall effect which is dependent upon the amount of oxide, the viscosity of the glaze, where it is placed, how it is applied, and the number of times it is fired.

Captain John Norton, whose pottery works was founded in 1793, was the pioneer of Bennington pottery. His works, operated by his descendants after he died, produced a great variety of wares for over a century until they closed in 1894. Christopher Webber Fenton, who married Norton's granddaughter, was the other key figure in the development of Bennington pottery. The Norton Company and the company with which Fenton was chiefly associated—the United States Pottery Company, which lasted from 1847 to 1858—are responsible for many innovations as well as for a prolific and varied output including not only the mottled-brown Rockingham type but Parian ware, flint enamel, graniteware, and yellowware, as well as porcelain and china.

Christopher Fenton wished to make Bennington the Staffordshire of America, and he succeeded in no small measure. The little Vermont hamlet became the center of experimentation with new clays and techniques. The great variety of items manufactured at the United States Pottery Company were featured in a special exhibit at the Crystal Palace Exhibition in London in 1851 and were seen at New York's Crystal Palace Exhibition in 1853. This display of Rockingham ware included pitchers, bowls, toilet sets, urns, vases, cuspidors, pedestals for flowerpots and statuary, columns, figures, lions, cows, and Toby mugs. Rockingham ware became so popular, especially after the impressive showing at the New York exhibit, that more than sixty American potteries manufactured it up until 1900.

Among the outstanding items in Rockingham ware were pitchers, Tobies, coachman bottles, lions, and poodle dogs. These objects were of English design, to which American potters added their own glazes and color. Daniel Greatbach, the master potter of Staffordshire, England, was brought over to work at the Henderson pottery works in Jersey City. In about 1843 he modeled a hound-handled pitcher that was then copied by most of the other potteries. Another pitcher modeled by this craftsman had a mask on the front of the spout, a hunting scene, and an American eagle pulling the tail of a British lion. He also made the "Apostle pitcher" displaying embossed figures of the Apostles within Gothic arches. Also of special interest to collectors of Rockingham is the "Rebekah at the Well" teapot modeled by Charles Coxon for the Baltimore pottery of Bennett and Brothers. It was copied from the design of an English porcelain jug.

269

270 Toby pitchers. Top shelf, left to right: dark Rockingham bank; flint enamel snuff jar; yellowware snuff jar; rare jar with tricorne hat; Rockingham snuff jar; green flint enamel snuff jar; Albany slip snuff jar. Middle shelf: Albany slip Toby bottle, also called Coachman bottle; two Rockingham bottles; rare stoneware bottle with cobalt blue decoration, dated 1849; three flint enamel bottles. Bottom shelf: two large and rare Zachary Taylor ''Rough and Ready'' pieces in Rockingham glaze, 1849; flint enamel jar with ''I'm a Brick'' inscription on hat. Photograph by Frank L. Forward, courtesy the Bennington Museum, Bennington, Vermont

271 *Many hundreds of different pitcher designs, shapes, and colors were produced in Bennington. Illustrated here are some of the most popular pieces. Top shelf: three pitchers marked "Norton and Fenton" and dated 1845 to 1847; from left to right: six-sided Rockingham pitcher called "Dark Lustre," yellowware pitcher, pitcher with lead glaze. Middle shelf: three variations of the hound-handled pitcher with grapevine on neck and collar and stag hunting scene on the body; middle pitcher is lead-glazed. Bottom shelf: tulip and heart pattern flint enamel pitcher, c. 1849–58; diamond pattern with brilliant green oxide streaks; flint enamel pitcher with alternate rib pattern. Photograph by Frank L. Forward, courtesy the Bennington Museum, Bennington, Vermont*

272

273

274

275

276

277

278

279

272 *Ewer with Robert Fulton steamboat, c. 1830–40* 273 *Rockingham pitcher probably made in Zanesville, Ohio, c. 1850–75* 274 *Rockingham pitcher made at the Salamander Works, New York, 1848* 275 *Rockingham pitcher, c. 1850* 276 *Pitcher made by J. E. Caire & Company, Poughkeepsie, New York, c. 1849* 277 *Rockingham pitcher made in Bennington, 1844* 278 *Pitcher made by Solomon Bell, Strasburg, Virginia, c. 1850* 279 *Pitcher made by Fenton at Bennington, 1849*

280

281

280 *Displayed on the open shelves of this Pennsylvania German pine cupboard of the eighteenth century are earthenware plates, jars, and jugs with slip and sgraffito decoration. Photograph courtesy the Henry Francis du Pont Winterthur Museum, Winterthur, Delaware*
281 *Covered earthenware dish of pierced work required extreme care in the cutting. Such work was often performed by potters who sought to impress their prospective employers with their skill* **282** *In this sugar bowl the lid has a unique decoration of many-tiered beaded flanges and scrolls* **283** *Covered jar from southeastern Pennsylvania shows the sgraffito treatment of conventional tulip-and-leaf design. Made in 1830*

To a Bit of Clay
They Added Beauty

282

PENNSYLVANIA GERMAN settlers from the Rhine Valley inherited a love for ornamental kitchenware which reflected Old World techniques and traditions. The abundance of native red clay, the endless supply of fuel, and the ease in setting up a kiln were ideally suited to the continuation of their pottery handicrafts.

Directly beneath the rich, fertile soil of eastern Pennsylvania, especially in Montgomery, Bucks, and Berks counties, a good quality of potter's clay was found. Once a potter located a supply, he stripped the top layer of soil to a depth of about six inches in an area about five by ten feet. The clay was then dug and hauled to a homemade kiln. When one clay pit was exhausted, the potter had no difficulty in finding another close at hand.

Kitchen articles were the first to be fashioned from this clay—plates, pots, bowls, and baking dishes. The potter also produced red roofing tiles, reminiscent of his European homeland, a practice that has continued into the twentieth century. All potters made nests of pots in graded sizes for apple butter and milk; covered earthenware jars for pickles and preserves; mixing bowls, jelly molds and colanders; and handled jugs for cider and vinegar, which were stoppered with corncob stumps. Many potters turned out red clay teapots,

dark-brown coffeepots, cups, thick mugs of quart capacity for ale or spirits, and pitchers in varying sizes. There were enormous platters in oval, round, or octagonal shapes and casseroles with ornamental covers.

The potter used two essentially related techniques to apply his patterns to the flat or rounded surface of his wares; slip decoration and sgraffito. Both methods have been known since ancient times, and descended into the hands of the Pennsylvania Germans by way of central European ceramic artisans. Slip decoration was applied by means of one or several goose quills that fed a thin clay fluid from a slip cup. The potter manipulated this cup deftly until the fluid flowed in scrolls, squiggles, or dots to delineate his design. The thin white or creamy solution was a special type of clay, or "slip," imported from New Jersey. As the potter worked his slip cup, his deft movements produced a calligraphic language, not unlike writing done with a broad-pointed nib. He was also able to make thin hairlines with which he would outline figures and decorations. Great skill was required in this operation, as the craftsman's strokes, once applied to the surface, were permanent. When fired, the slip became a light cream or buff color, which contrasted with the darker background of the base.

283

284   285

286   287

The second method of decorating pottery surfaces is sgraffito, a term derived from the Italian *sgraffiare*, "to scratch." This technique was used extensively by the Pennsylvania German potters and involves incising a design into a semiwet clay surface by means of a thin sharp-edged wooden tool. First a cream or golden-yellow slip color was applied, then the hairline design was scratched through it, exposing the rust color of the redware; then the piece was fired. The potter worked to achieve a simplicity and clarity of expression —every line, floral form, bird, or figure was rendered with a minimum of strokes.

288

289

290

291

284–291 *Slip-decorated ware was made by trickling liquid clay, called slip, through a quill attached to a cup, and required a sure sense of design and direction. True slip is usually distinguished by light-colored ornamentation upon a darker ground, the resultant design taking on a light relief. In contrast, sgraffito ware is the result of incising lines into the soft clay surface before firing. The lines thus depressed, or intaglioed, show dark against a white or yellowish field. Slipware plates are 284, 285, 288, 289; sgraffito-ware pieces are 286, 287, 290, 291*

Decorated Tin & Toleware

293

BY THE CLOSE of the eighteenth century, several tin centers had been established in New England. Boston, as the chief Colonial seaport, was the place where tinplate imported from England arrived. The plates, generally ten by fourteen inches, arrived in wooden boxes, and were transported by horse or oxen to tin shops throughout the countryside. One of the better known and most prosperous tin shops was established in Berlin, Connecticut, by the Pattison brothers from Ireland. Zachariah Stevens, trained as a blacksmith, abandoned this trade for the more lucrative practice of tinsmithing. He set up a shop at Stevens Plains, near Portland, Maine, and his business eventually prospered to the point where eleven shops were in operation under his direction. Oliver Filley, a former peddler in Vermont, began to manufacture tinware in 1800 and subsequently opened three branch operations to meet the demand for his products. The Butler

family ran a successful shop in Greenville, New York, where various family members made, painted, and decorated a complete line of tinware. In addition to these personally directed ventures, tinware factories were in operation in Albany, New York, and in Litchfield and Clinton, Connecticut.

The tinsmith, or "whitesmith," as he was called to distinguish his trade from that of the blacksmith, required few tools other than hardwood mallets, shears, and molds to pattern his beaten forms. Later, to supplement his crude utensils, he acquired some simple machinery, such as a roller, crimper, edger, and power-operated shears. When extra helpers were needed, they were brought over from England, where the tinware industry had been firmly established, and both makers and decorators had practiced the art for generations. If the tinsmith sought to build up his trade beyond his community, he took to the road in a wagon filled with his wares, which

294

292 *On the open shelves of this pine dresser is a collection of decorated nineteenth-century tinware including teapots, pitchers, beakers, plates, trays, and other utensils. The vivid coloring of the freehand brush strokes and the spontaneity of the compositions reveal their rural origins in the Pennsylvania German regions and New England. Photograph courtesy the Henry Francis du Pont Winterthur Museum, Winterthur, Delaware* **293** *Can for delivering water to wash basins. Hand painting is further assisted by transfer inserts from decalcomania designs, c. 1870* **294** *Slop pail, companion piece to the watering can*

295

296

included pans, teapots and coffeepots, colanders, graters, cookie cutters, canisters, trays, candlestick holders, and small toys fashioned out of scraps. Light tinplate was used for decorative articles; wares designed for cooking or baking were made of heavy tinplate. The Yankee peddler soon became a regular visitor to farms at a distance from convenient shopping centers. As early as 1800, consumer preferences dictated the market for goods in all categories, whether plain tinware for cooking utensils or fancier goods—hand painted, stencil decorated, or japanned. Tinware varied considerably in price and fell into three classifications: inexpensive articles with a minimum of decoration called "painted tin"; moderately priced goods known as "japanned ware"; and the more expensive decorated pieces called

295–300 *The large surface of trays presented an opportunity to design, improvise, and otherwise express a love of ornamentation. A particularly pleasing composition is shown in 295, in which fountain, flowers, and leaf forms—further amplified with an abundance of delicate tendrils—combine to produce an inspired garden fantasy, made c. 1850. Totally different in design and feeling is the "coffin tray" for bread or cake, typical of Pennsylvania German motifs, shown in 296. The Chippendale tray with*

297

298

"tole," from the French *tôle peinte*, meaning painted tinware.

Generally, decorated toleware had a black background on which the colors were opaquely applied in one of two techniques. One method called for stenciling through cutout areas, the open spaces, cut from stiff cardboard or thin sheet metal, serving as a template for the colors. The other method involved hand painting directly onto the surface, either freehand or following drawn guide lines. The black backgrounds were painted with asphaltum, a brownish-black substance mixed with varnish. It produced a rich, velvety surface that was particularly durable after firing and had a magnetic affinity for gold leaf—one of the reasons it was favored for toleware and furniture painting.

299

300

piecrust rolled edge, 297 and 300, broke away from traditional rectangular and oval shapes. In 297 naturalistically represented flower and leaf forms are geometrically positioned, while 300, c. 1840, includes a stenciled rendition of one of the first trains. The tin tray in 298 has a series of striped borders with formalized floral designs repeating around four sides. The deep apple dish, 299, was painted by Zachariah Stevens, Portland, Maine, c. 1810–20

301

302

301–307 *The coloration of various tinware and toleware objects shows a great variety of treatments, although certain colors predominate. Where the background color is not black, crimson, vermilion, and coffee-brown are preferred. A few yellows may also be seen. Floral motifs call for reds and golds, and petal forms for dark emerald greens; blues appear sparingly. White accents occur in bands and elsewhere as chiaroscuro highlights. Aging contributes to the overall effect, as the darkening of leaf forms and the patina acquired by the bright colors plus the flecking of tin at the corners combine to produce a blend that is altogether pleasing*

303

304

305

306

307

308

308 *Gilded iron weather vane with the Angel Gabriel blowing a trumpet presents an unusually handsome silhouette. The figure of Gabriel was a popular subject for weather vanes well into the nineteenth century. Made by Gould and Hazlett, Boston, in 1840* **309** *Wrought-iron weather vane with gilded banner and finial, one of the oldest extant American vanes. Made by a local smith in 1673 for the first church in Concord, Massachusetts*

North, East, South, West

ANDRONICUS, A GREEK astronomer living about 100 B.C., created the first recorded weather vane when he hoisted a bronze figure of Triton atop his Tower of Winds in Athens. The winds were worshiped as oracles for good or evil, and the adage "An ill wind that blows no good" was scarcely an empty metaphor. Early Scandinavian seafarers used vanes on their ships to help predict the weather. In ninth-century Europe, the pope decreed that the rooster should be placed on top of churches as a religious symbol to ward off evil and as evidence of good faith. The cock that crowed thrice to the apostle Peter prevailed throughout the Middle Ages not only for its religious significance but also for its functional and decorative value. These ideas were inherited by the early Colonists, who followed European examples in their vanes. The rooster, because of its association with traditions in Christendom, became the predominant motif used atop barns and houses. At first the weathercocks were cut from flat wooden boards or sheet iron, but as early as 1656 a handsome copper cockerel graced the Dutch Reformed Church in Albany. An Indian weather vane of hammered copper for the Province House in Boston was the work of "Deacon" Shem Drowne, a craftsman and metalworker noted for his mantelpiece carvings, figureheads, and trade signs. The chanticleer vane taken from the Fitch Tavern at New Bedford, Massachusetts, is an outstanding example of the early wooden, painted board type. Gracefully styled with a long curved neck and a sweep of its back and tail, it is almost four feet

tall. (Also from the hand of Drowne is the unusual and celebrated grasshopper vane dated 1742 that still tops the cupola of Faneuil Hall in Boston—a design duplicated a century later by the Cushing Company of Waltham, Massachusetts, whose copies are highly prized by collectors.)

The artistic treatment of the rooster motif in vanes varies greatly with the local craftsman. Without pictorial sources for guidance, each farmer or carpenter fashioned his own weathercock. The outer silhouette, cutout areas, and the arrangement and grouping of tail feathers attest to the creative ability of the folk artists, who exhibited a flair for functional design and a native vitality difficult to match in their purity of line and expression. In later years, however, the weathercock lost much of its grace and originality, becoming chunkier and more realistic; perhaps this was brought about by its changing from a quasi-religious to a secular role. This contrast is particularly noticeable if one studies the catalogues of weather-vane manufacturers issued in the second half of the nineteenth century, for their realistic zinc- and copper-stamped roosters have lost all traces of the unique design qualities that typified the handiwork of the farmers who had originally fashioned them.

It would be difficult to find an artifact in which design variants outnumber those of the weather vane. Personal tastes, regional economy, and the materials employed account for this variety. In agricultural communities, farmers preferred weather vanes in the form of a cow, horse, sheep, or pig—in addition, of course, to the cockerel—while in seacoast towns, houses and barns are marked with cod,

309

123

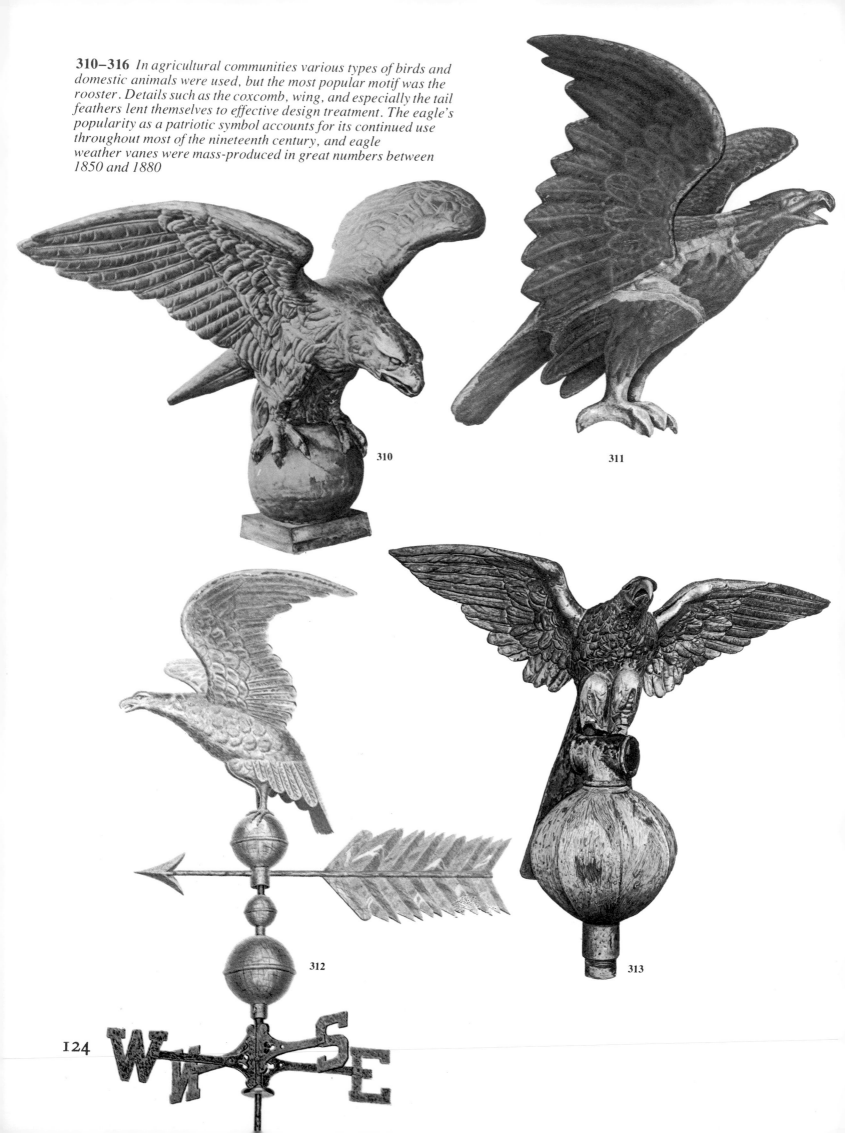

310–316 *In agricultural communities various types of birds and domestic animals were used, but the most popular motif was the rooster. Details such as the coxcomb, wing, and especially the tail feathers lent themselves to effective design treatment. The eagle's popularity as a patriotic symbol accounts for its continued use throughout most of the nineteenth century, and eagle weather vanes were mass-produced in great numbers between 1850 and 1880*

310

311

312

313

swordfish, seagulls, whales, dolphins, and sailboats. Other occupational designs were also featured: a firehouse displayed a vane with a fireman blowing his trumpet or a fire engine; a train station was surmounted by a vane with a locomotive. Many tradesmen found that the weather vane provided an opportunity to call attention to their wares and services. A butcher, for example, advertised with a pig being dragged to market; a woolen textile factory displayed a sheep or ram; a shipbuilder

314

315

featured a two-masted schooner; and a race-track exhibited a horse-drawn sulky and rider. Thus the weather vane, in addition to its functional purpose, took on the character of a trade symbol.

The eagle in many poses and attitudes, crouching or with outstretched wings, appeared in weather vanes of wood or sheet metal and in castings. Although patriotic feelings were asserted following the Revolution and during the early Federal period, it was not until the 1850s that the eagle motif was widely used. In most eagle weather vanes, the native instincts of the individual craftsman, unhampered by rules of heraldry or tradition, resulted in freedom of expression.

Other national emblems appeared in lesser numbers. Miss Columbia and Miss Liberty survive in a few well-preserved examples; Uncle Sam appeared in a few instances. Flags,

316

317

318

ribbons, pennants, and bannerets, all useful appendages with decorative potential, were made in wrought iron or copper. One writer, expressing the difference that developed between American and European weather vanes, summarizes the American tradition by calling it "a new and ingratiating heraldry, a heraldry of democracy."

317 *Cow weather vanes used atop barn cupolas did not appear until the late nineteenth century* **318** *Fish weather vane —here with a glass eye—a motif limited to the eastern seaboard and especially New England* **319** *Indian weather vane, hollow copper, c. 1850* **320–322** *Running horse, a highly popular weather-vane motif, c. 1870–1900* **323** *Horse-drawn sulky and driver weather vane, sometimes used to indicate the breed of racing horse housed in a barn, and a more distinctive symbol than the horse alone, c. 1875*

319

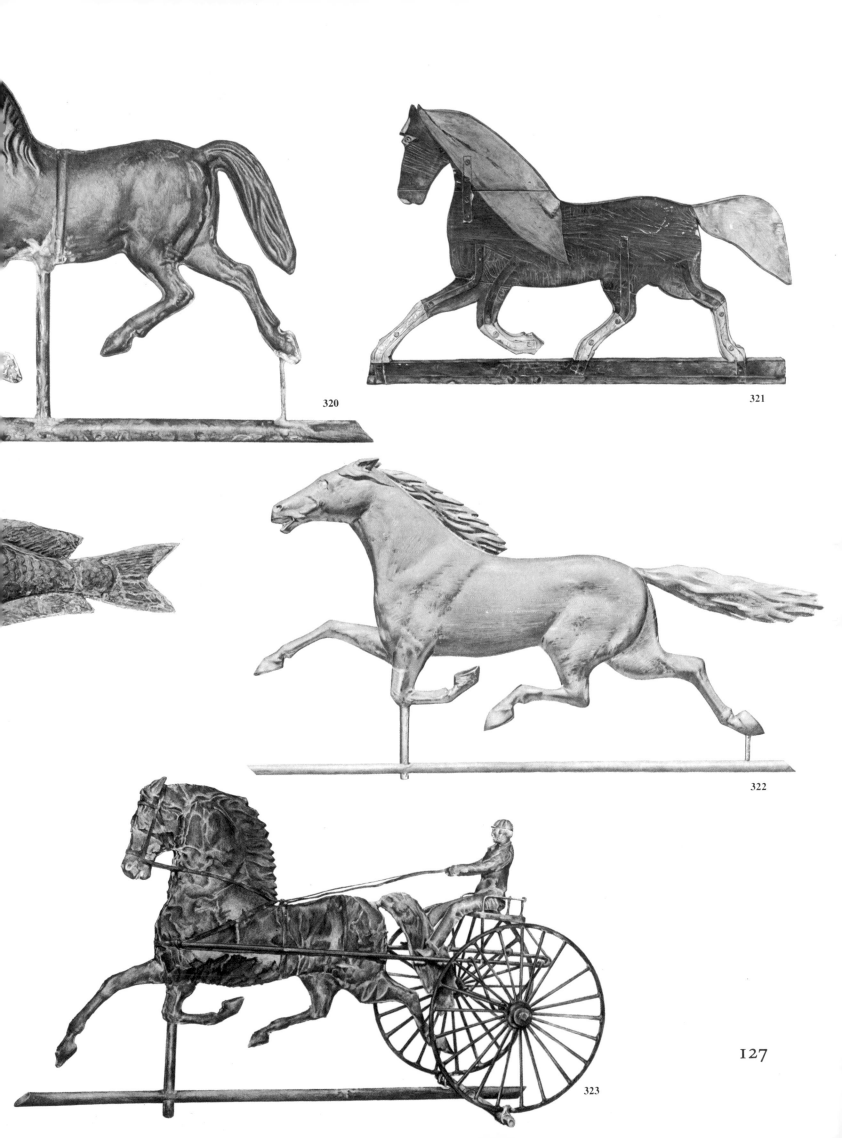

320

321

322

323

Bandboxes for Milady's Bonnets

325

PAPER-COVERED BANDBOXES for ladies and hatboxes for men were lightweight traveling adjuncts that have no exact equivalent today. On the Continent, during the eighteenth century, bandboxes were used to transport and store elaborately starched ruffs and other personal finery. When the ruff lost its appeal and was replaced with the soft lace collar, the bandbox remained a popular and convenient repository. Ladies found it ideal for storing and transporting jewelry, ribbons, artificial flowers, hairpieces, and a myriad of bagatelles. These early boxes were so delicately constructed and fragile that it is surprising that any have survived the century and a half since they were first fashionable in the United States. However, when yesteryear's travelers boarded coaches for perilous overland journeys, they clung tenaciously to their bandboxes, not entrusting them to coachmen; this habit and the fact that many of them were stored in dry attics may account for their survival.

The American bandbox boom started during the second quarter of the nineteenth century, paralleling the development of new means of travel. However, the earliest colored papers for these boxes were probably imported, most of the finely decorated ones coming from France and England. When the box fad gained momentum, the domestic paper printer, using woodblocks, began to design gay and boldly colored papers rather than waiting for the latest imported designs. The earliest use of wallpaper-covered boxes is noted in an advertisement of 1789 by John Fisher of Baltimore, and a fragment of paper from a bandbox owned by Abigail Adams is preserved in the Cooper-Hewitt Museum in New York, noted for its large bandbox collection.

Most bandbox factories were located in the larger cities. New York, Philadelphia, Boston, and Hartford boasted about thirty of these plants. However, the vogue for bandboxes did not last, and most of these factories were out of business by mid-century. The passing of the stagecoach era and the growth in travel by boat and train called for stouter luggage. Hatboxes which could hold half a dozen hats were made of heavier fabric and reinforced construction, and leather luggage, which could better withstand rough handling at depots, was preferred. Thus the bandbox, which had seen its best days, gradually faded into oblivion.

324 *Array of bandboxes stacked in a bandbox room, a common adjunct to a millinery shop in cities and large towns during the second quarter of the nineteenth century. Photograph by Einmars J. Mengis, courtesy Shelburne Museum, Shelburne, Vermont* 325 *Octagonal bandbox, more costly than oval or circular boxes, since the corners had to be especially reinforced*

◄ 324

326

327

328

329

330

331

332

333

326–336 *Paper coverings for bandboxes were either all-over patterns, usually floral, or scenic designs, in which case the motif was tailored to fit around the box. The former were more easily adapted to the box surface, being used for both sides and top with only the addition of an edging on the lid. Scenic designs were printed on a long strip of paper from wooden blocks and then glued on, with the seam at the back. Typical scenic designs include: ''Windmill Railroad,'' 327, commemorating the advent of the railroad (c. 1830); scenes of rural life, 328 (c. 1830), and 335 (c. 1835); 334, log cabin with riverboat and sunburst (c. 1840); and 336, a handsome public building, here an asylum for the deaf and dumb*

334

335

336

337

Hand-hooked for the Home

338

MAKING RUGS from scraps, strings, and bits of wool and yarn woven together according to personal taste was one of the crafts allocated to the household. The rugs showed the creative instinct of the cottage dweller, and for the long hours of painstaking detail there was a noble satisfaction when the final stitches were put in place.

Experts seem to agree that the art of hooking rugs is an American development, originating in the northeastern section of New England and in the neighboring maritime provinces of Canada. It was brought to these shores by the Scandinavians. The French, English, Welsh, and Scots adopted it during the latter part of the eighteenth century. A long period of gestation occurred; few examples appeared much before 1820. The technique of hooking may be traced to the old method of "thrumming," that is, "of fastening thrums, short cut-off pieces of yarn or cloth, to a background of fabric so as to give a heavy nap. This was usually accomplished by poking the thrums through holes or mesh, so that the two ends showed on one side." The background material was either homespun linen, factory-woven cotton, or burlap. Cloth strips were cut from leftover woolens or scraps, and a metal hook was used to draw the strips through the background fabric into loops. The loops were either cut or left uncut and their length determined the softness of the pile.

Early hooked rugs show an engaging naiveté of design. With no academic art training, rugmakers ventured into a field involving artistic decisions. The rug area became a canvas on which design, form, color, and texture were combined with skillful needlework to produce a picture. The designer was called on to exercise taste at every turn, a test of blending artistry with manual dexterity.

337 *Universally acknowledged to be one of the rarest of all early American handmade carpets, the famous Caswell rug at the Metropolitan Museum of Art in New York City is an object lesson in native handcrafts. It was made in Castleton, Vermont, in 1835 by Zeruah Higley Guernsey and became known as the "Caswell Carpet" because of her subsequent marriage to Mr. Caswell in 1846. Often referred to as the "Blue Cat Rug" because of a whimsical book about it, it is made up of numerous squares embroidered in what was called "double Kensington stitch," on firm homespun. Its floral motifs, birds and cats, fruits and foliage reveal an exuberant spirit. The portion shown here represents about a quarter of the rug; some two years were spent in the making, from shearing the wool to the dyeing and final embroidery. Its design is a treasure trove of homely inspiration in the best native tradition of needlecraft* 338 *The bridal couple, only one of almost eighty squares, is a complete, self-contained gem in the Caswell carpet, one of many*

339–343 *Florals are favorites. The universal appeal of flowers, their profusion of color, and the ease with which they can be drawn and hooked account for floral popularity in the design of hooked rugs. The more successful rugs involve a schematic plan such as those in which an outer arrangement forms a border, as in 340 and 343, or a series of concentric ovals, as in 339*

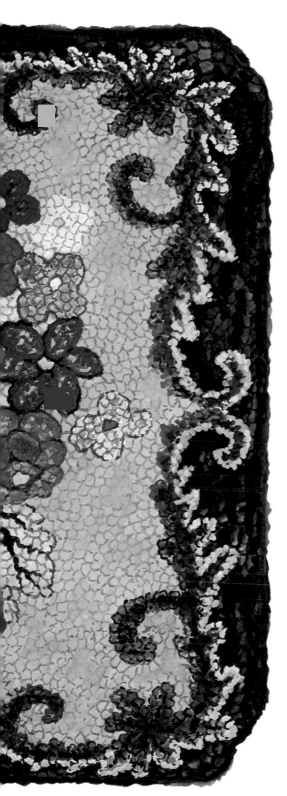

342

343

Floral motifs, in formal or informal arrangements, loose sprays, garlands, and festoons used as either central medallions or border offered almost unlimited potential for originality. The floral bouquet has been the dominant design theme of thousands of hooked rugs, and the free interpretation of the floral forms often resulted in young, fresh designs. Many hundred-year-old hooked rugs look as if they have just emerged from the studios or workshops of today's avant-garde artists.

Heirlooms from Old Looms

345

THOSE WHO SPIN and weave by hand find themselves part of the continuity of history, as textile processes are among the oldest and most important inventions of ancient man. To this continuous record, the women of America have made a lasting contribution. From the earliest days to well into the nineteenth century, Colonial women, starting with the shearings of sheep and the cuttings of flax, wove the coarse fibers into articles of beauty and utility.

Hand spinning is the process of converting fibers into a form of yarn, thread, or string. The best-known animal fibers in Colonial America came from sheep and rabbit fur. The only vegetable fibers grown were flax and hemp. Yarn was a loosely spun fiber, while thread designated a fiber more tightly spun and twisted. More accurately, the product of man's earliest attempts to make thread may be described as string, which resulted from separating fibers with the fingers and twisting them into the strength or thickness needed. Without

344 *Eighteenth-century loom on which the home weaver made her homespun bedspreads, coverlets, floor runners, and other materials was a crudely built affair, yet substantial enough to withstand the continual stresses of the weaving process. The professional weaver, working in his shop, used the same general type of loom. His, however, was equipped with more harnesses—from four to as many as twelve. Photograph courtesy Colonial Williamsburg*
345 *Ever-popular rose motif in symmetrical design scheme, c. 1840*   **346, 347** *Woven on Jacquard looms, these coverlets are typical; large central area carries borders on four sides of the bedspreads, c. 1835–40*

346

347

348

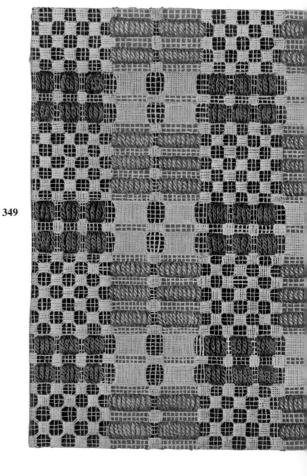

348–350 *Pure geometric patterns result in an infinite number of variations as produced in the overshot technique of weaving. Dark wool lies on the light warp, skipping a number of threads; hence the name "overshot." Heavy weft threads and thin warp produce an uneven surface, so that there are textural as well as pattern variants*

349

spinning there could be no weaving; without fibers there could be no spinning. Fortunately, early laws produced an abundance of the basics for spinning and weaving. In Massachusetts, for example, an ordinance of the 1640s made it compulsory for each Colonial family to spin a given quantity of yarn every year or face a penalty of heavy fines. Growing flax and raising sheep were urgent economic necessities. At home the making of cloth was both essential and inevitable. Sir Henry Moore, governor of New York in the 1760s, wrote: "Every house swarms with children who are set to work as soon as they are able to Spin and Card, and as every family is furnished with a Loom, Itinerant Weavers then put the finishing hand on the work."

In every Colonial home there was the sound of the whirling spinning wheel. To prepare wool for the high, or "walking," wheel on which it was spun into yarn, the heavy winter fleece of the sheep was processed through an arduous succession of cleaning, carding, and combing. The spinning was done on a large wheel; flax was spun on a smaller wheel, also known as a Saxon wheel, a tiring chore often performed by the man of the house. The

desired flax fibers were separated by soaking, pounding, scraping, or combing. After the woolen yarn was spun, it was wound into hanks on a wooden frame called a niddy noddy, about two feet long.

The large loom on which the yarns or threads were woven into cloth was usually the work of the local carpenter. It occupied a space in the attic, a separate shed, or a special loom room. When space was at a premium the contrivance, sometimes built by the master of the house, was placed in the kitchen, where it occupied about the area of a four-poster bed. The mysteries of weaving—of warp and woof, of heddle and shuttle—were carried on for long hours in order to produce the simple fabrics needed to clothe the members of the family, or to provide the basic material for all bedding and coverlets.

In the early Colonial period, all cloth required by the average family was made by the housewife, with the help of the children. Later, a great deal of weaving was carried on by traveling journeymen. (The term derived from the fact that the "journey" represented a day's work; in other words, these craftsmen were paid a day's wages.) They relieved the housewife of her tedious weaving and also

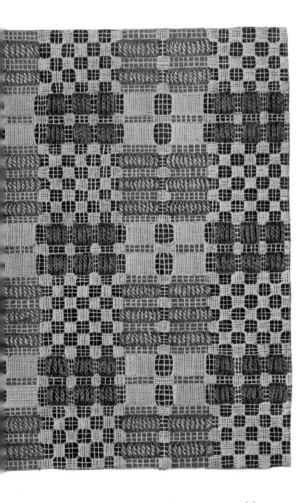

helped somewhat in pottery making, carpentry, tailoring, and various other crafts. They were an enlivening influence throughout the Colonies, and were depended upon to supply vivid gossip about neighbors and other places. Finally, the weaving shop and the professional weaver became a part of each community, and women ordered fabrics from the weaver though they still furnished him with yarn.

The fancy flowered coverlets, the Jacquard, include some of the most magnificent designs in the field of American weaving. These first appeared around 1820, particularly in New York and Pennsylvania, later spreading westward into Ohio, Kentucky, Indiana, and Illinois. It is the opinion of most students that the early examples were produced by professional weavers on the draw loom, while later ones were made on hand-operated looms with the aid of the Jacquard attachment. Featured in this general type of coverlet was a wide variety of floral motifs, employed both in diapered arrangements and freely chosen groupings of roses and tulips, laurel, and other leafy ornaments. The borders on the drop sides of these spreads were elaborate and striking, utilizing many finely rendered patriotic motifs. There were stars, shields, eagles, ribbons, mottoes, and figures of George Washington, as well as Mount Vernon and the Capitol. Accompanying these were strong chauvinistic urgings: "United We Stand, Divided We Fall," "Under this eagle, we prosper," "Agriculture & Manufactures Are the Foundation of our Independence." It was customary for the weaver to place the date and his name, or that of the individual for whom the coverlet was made, in a corner.

350

351

351 The Quilting Party, *painted by an unknown artist, c. 1840–50. It pictures an important social event: the final sewing into place of the many blocks and friendship pieces of the quilt. It was an occasion for festive animation, a time for the gathering of young and old in meetinghouse or schoolroom. Courtesy the Abby Aldrich Rockefeller Folk Art Collection, Williamsburg, Virginia* **352** *The spinning wheel was a fixture in every Colonial home. After the winter fleece was sheared from the sheep's back, it was processed through many stages of cleaning, carding, and combing. Then the loose fibers were deftly twisted at the wheel into continuous strands for weaving* **353** *Quilts were made up of units like this, sewn together for a large bedspread. This is a mosaic calico piece, made in 1810 near Corning, New York*

352

The Quilting Bee

NO WOMAN EVER quilted alone if she could help it. The quilting bee provided an opportunity for women to gather and gossip. When the bee was held in a grange hall or church vestry room, as many as twelve women could attend. Usually, however, the number of guests was limited to seven, who, with the hostess, made up two quilting frames, the equivalent of two tables of bridge. Good quilting in earlier times was a social requisite, and it behooved the ambitious woman to be an expert with her needle.

The quilting frame was a simple homemade affair, much like today's curtain stretcher. The frame held the patchwork securely so that the decorative top quilt, the inner lining of cotton or wool, and the backing could be sewn together. The quilt was "rolled" from each of the four sides until the center was reached and the quilt completed. Often several quilts were finished in a single session which lasted all day. These sessions ended with a supper of roast chicken or turkey. The men usually arrived in time for the feast, after which there followed singing and dancing. Like so many well-established rural customs—apple-paring bees, corn-husking contests, and barn-raising parties—the traditional quilting party carried with it

all of the social amenities. The event marked the successful completion of many months of laborious handiwork.

Several forms of coverlet were derived from European backgrounds; they followed traditional patterns and displayed regional variations. The patchwork quilt, however, made from cotton, calico, and silk fragments, was a distinctly American invention—an economic necessity. The need to salvage every scrap of material and to piece these scraps together to form attractive patterns of beauty and ingenuity constituted an original folk art. Whereas affluent women could import bolts of English materials or patronize specialty shops, those with limited resources had to improvise, making patterns from their carefully hoarded remnants. These are the prized heirlooms in today's needlecraft collections.

Toward the middle of the nineteenth century, the social aspects of quilting and the popularity of quilting parties resulted in group needlecraft for the making of signature, friendship, autograph, bride, album, and presentation quilts. Each quilt was generally intended for a special person or special occasion and conveyed the sentiments of the well-wishers. The donor or originator of the quilt planned the basic outline and assigned separate blocks

353

141

354

354, 355 *The Star of Bethlehem, an intriguing pattern involving difficult piecing and endless patience, has had great attraction for oldtime quilt makers. The making of the star called for thousands of diamond-shaped pieces of chintz, calico, and copperplate fabrics, carefully chosen for color blending and harmony. The eight-pointed star had four corners and four triangles to be designed and pieced according to personal whims, but the dominant motif of the Star held real fascination*

to friends in the group. When the blocks were completed, the group gathered for a sociable afternoon to assemble the quilt, with its embroidered signatures or good wishes. The honored guest might have been a minister or his wife, an esteemed citizen, or a bride. The variety of designs and expressions of a dozen or more women produced a most interesting memento. The interrelationship of the separate pieces created an ensemble of rare loveli-

ness, quite revealing as an exercise in original folk arts and crafts.

A study of the more intricate appliquéd quilts will show why years often went into their making. Smaller units like the Orange Peel, Caesar's Crown, Basket of Tulips, Little Red Schoolhouse, or, for that matter, any unit repeated forty or fifty times for the quilt's central area involved the most work. The completion of such a quilt could easily have taken hundreds of hours. During the Civil War and the period that followed, there was a decline in quilt making. The introduction of machinery in the textile industry eliminated the need for such tedious needlework. The friendship quilt and its sentiments, along with woven coverlets and appliquéd masterpieces, became treasured heirlooms, testaments to a folk art that has all but vanished.

356

356 *Floral wreath, horn of plenty, and basket of flowers are further embellished with the introduction of the flag and eagle, pineapple, Bible, doves, and lyres—a complete grammar of decoration expressing the sentimental lore of mid-nineteenth-century life* **357–362** *Squares of calico show the simple elements of which large spreads were composed* **363** *Floral wreaths, always popular, enabled the quilt maker to express her love of color and imagination in a garden fantasy* **364** *Basket of flowers, a perennial favorite in patterns, arranged with geometric simplicity*

357

358

359

360

361

362

363

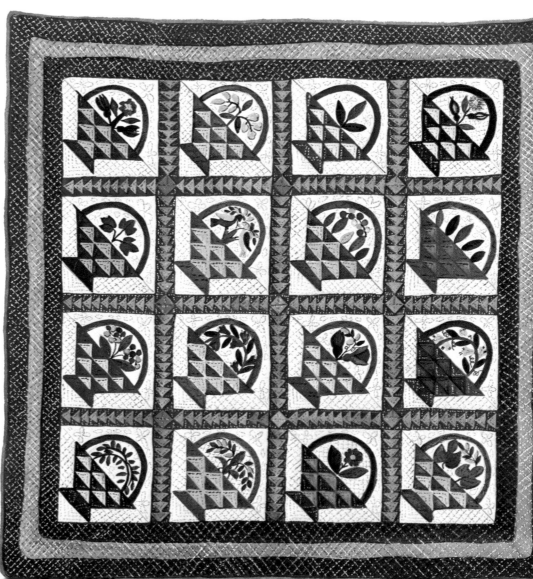

364

365

365 The Circus *was painted in 1874 by A. Logan, National Gallery of Art, Washington, D.C. Gift of Edgar William and Bernice Chrysler Garbisch* **366** *The circus wagon* The Golden Age of Chivalry, *designed by George Lawrence of the Sebastian Wagon Company, was built c. 1887–89*

The Circus Comes to Town

366

"HURRY! HURRY! HURRY!" has been the raucous cry of the big-top barker ever since John Robinson hauled the first traveling show, consisting of three wagons, five horses, and a tent, beyond the Alleghenies in 1824. Before the nineteenth century ended, the American circus had become not only "The Greatest Show on Earth" but a big business which involved dozens of touring troupes, thousands of performers, and animals from all parts of the globe. This was the heyday of the circus, roughly from 1875 to 1915, with its dazzling three rings, its freaks, and its spangles, glitter, and noise.

The magnificent prologue to the main show was the mile-long parade in a slow, well-ordered procession from the railroad yards to the big tent. The brightly decorated circus wagons carried clowns, musicians, lady performers, and animal cages. The steam calliopes sounded a brassy cacophony, and the clumsy, ten-ton *Two Hemispheres* wagon was drawn by a team of forty horses, while dozens of elephants, from midget to jumbo, marched linked together tail in trunk. Phineas T. Barnum inaugurated this parade of colorful circus wagons with the attendant ballyhoo.

Favorite parade themes included allegories, legendary heroes of the golden age of chivalry, and Orientalia.

The few remaining circus wagons found today in museums and circus collections are reminders of those spectacles. These ponderous show pieces were created for glamour and showmanship; the over-ornamentation and excessive use of gilded scrolls were designed to captivate the eye Yet beneath the tinsel and gilt were finely carved figures, symbols of the circus during its apogee. While the whole town usually turned out to see the "supercolossal, transcendentally amazing and electrifying feats of the most stupendous exhibition ever exploited," the gaudy show wagons bore silent testimony to the skills of wood-carvers and gilders.

Wood-carving served a special function in the circus world. The wood-carver, working on contract, turned out wagons with little of the glamour associated with a wood sculptor. The carvings on the wagons were not intended to be studied closely, but were designed primarily as a part of the passing spectacle. They reflected the influences that produced the eclectic and Baroque decorations of that day. Most circus carving was the work of untrained

367

artists; it was not folk art but "popular art." The lavishly ornamented, highly colored wagons stimulated the visual senses and were the keynote of a transient style.

In the construction of the wagons, oak and hickory were used for the structural members and frames and yellow pine and whitewood for most of the carvings. The softer woods were more vulnerable to exposure; this played great havoc with the carved figures, resulting in splitting, cracking, and the loss of arms, fingers, and noses. It is surprising, therefore,

that any of these figures have survived. Van Amburgh's *Great Golden Chariot* was among the most lavish wagons. It was a richly carved structure which featured a helmeted, steel-armored noble slaying a lion with his lance, surrounded by Romanesque scrolls. The Colmar brothers' prize wagon had a lifesize nude on each corner; these gilded showgirls never failed to create a stir in the audience. The Wallace Circus had a steam calliope with a high driver's seat flanked by ornate scrolls from which emerged a female figure driving

367 *The circus wagon* United States *is one of the most magnificent examples of circus carving, replete with symbols of the American spirit. Figures and allegories proudly display the flag and the eagle. In the central panel the Goddess of Liberty stands flanked by Indian maidens. Every square foot is covered with architectural framework, arches and pilasters, arabesques and storied details designed to instill patriotic fervor in the hearts of spectators, c. 1875* **368** *Seated lion carved in relief for a Sparks circus wagon, c. 1900* **369** *Relief carving of figure with pipes of Pan, from circus wagon, c. 1900*

368

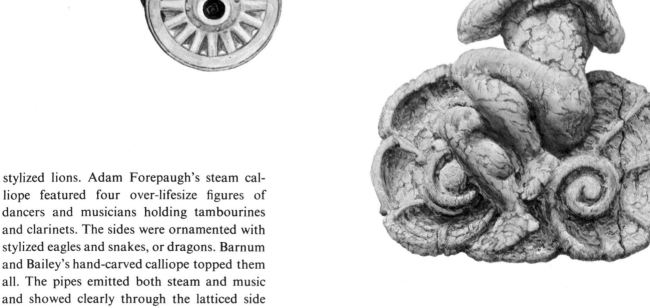

369

stylized lions. Adam Forepaugh's steam calliope featured four over-lifesize figures of dancers and musicians holding tambourines and clarinets. The sides were ornamented with stylized eagles and snakes, or dragons. Barnum and Bailey's hand-carved calliope topped them all. The pipes emitted both steam and music and showed clearly through the latticed side panels, which had elliptical center medallions surmounted by carved cherubs riding on the spread-winged birds.

370

371

150

Merry-Go-Round Menagerie

372

THE FIRST REVOLVING platform with the carrousel figures we know today was built in the little town of North Tonawanda, New York, in 1879. The improvements, which included elaborate ornamentation and fanciful animals, heralded a new era. Previously, merry-go-rounds had featured only prancing horses and chariot seats. Carrousels, an entertainment feature of every fair here and abroad, were also an essential part of the circus, and they became the major attraction in amusement parks throughout the country, their numbers expanding rapidly during the closing years of the nineteenth century. Almost a dozen companies were kept busy turning out a veritable menagerie of wooden figures.

Softwoods, especially white and yellow pine, were most suitable for the carrousel animals. Pine was easily worked, and greater

speed of execution meant the figures could be produced quickly in great numbers. Little sanding or polishing was necessary in the detailing of the head, mane, and tail portions. The rounded areas of the body which required sanding were turned over to assistants and apprentices. Finally, the figure was ready for painting and gilding. These carrousel animals received the same bright-colored treatment as the circus wagons. Frequent refurbishing was necessary to maintain their attractiveness, and often much of the original intention of the artist was obscured.

Bob Crandle, a wood-carver with a small factory on Third Avenue at Thirtieth Street in New York, specialized in hobbyhorses, velocipedes, and merry-go-round horses. The horse bodies were made from large pine-tree trunks, while the limbs were carved separately and doweled into position. Painting produced a

370, 371 *Carrousel figures of a rooster and a lion. Photographs courtesy the Smithsonian Institution, Washington, D.C. Eleanor and Mabel van Alstyne Collection*   **372, 373** *Galloping animals seemed more popular with older children, while the very young felt safer with the static figures. Deer and rabbit, c. 1890*

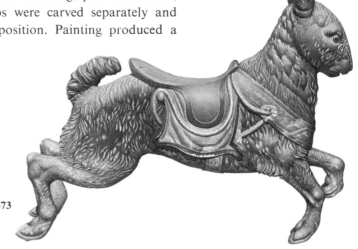

373

374–381 *The galloping steed was the carrousel's most popular animal, even though some of the more dangerous animals like lions and tigers attracted the daring youngsters. Stirrups were provided, but two- and three-year-olds had to be hoisted into their saddles by parents, who stood alongside. American carrousels with revolving platforms first appeared in 1879. Made in North Tonawanda, New York, between 1880 and 1900*

374

375

376

377

variety of equine figures; some were spotted to look like piebald horses and pintos, or even striped to look like zebras. Crandle also carved some lions and giraffes.

The horse was by far the most popular carrousel animal. It was treated in a variety of colorings to imitate the pinto, sorrel, palomino or the spotted white charger, a favorite among young riders. Lions, tigers, giraffes, dogs, roosters, ostriches, and many other exotic members of the menagerie appeared on the colorful carrousels.

378

379

380

381

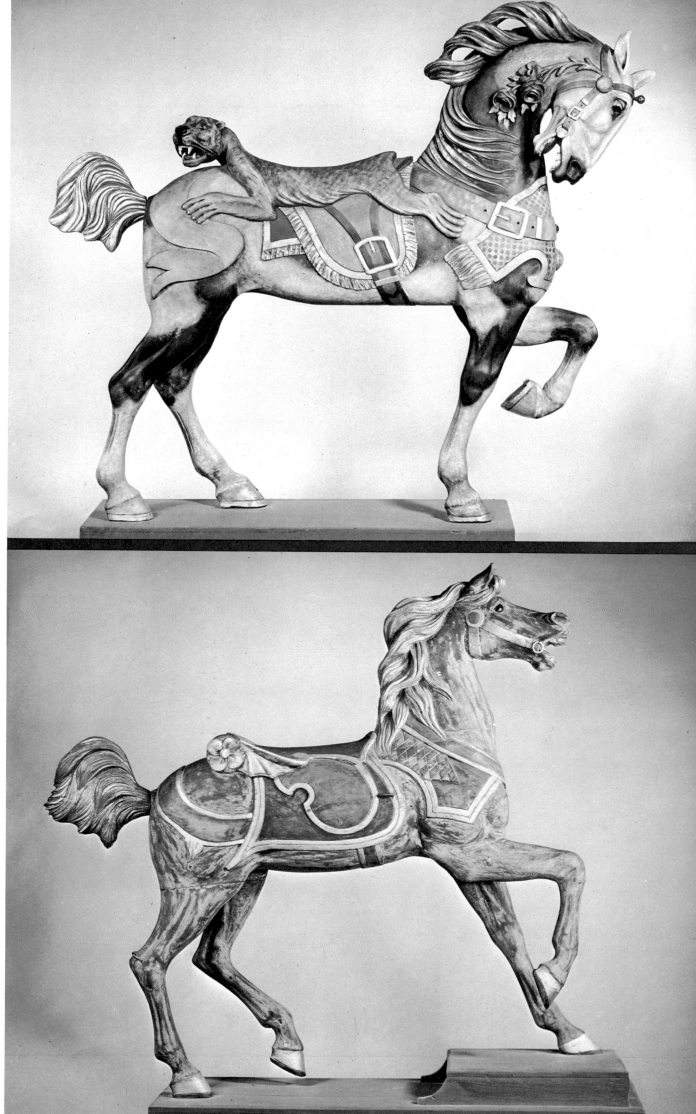

382

383

154

382, 383 *Carrousel horses, late nineteenth century. Photographs courtesy The Smithsonian Institution, Washington, D.C. Eleanor and Mabel van Alstyne Collection* **384** *Carrousel pig from Newport, Rhode Island* **385** *Carrousel rooster from Vermont, c. 1875–1900* **386** *Carrousel giraffe from Riverside, Rhode Island, c. 1888* **387** *Carrousel dog by Charles Looff, c. 1880*

384

385

386

387

388

389

388 The Hobby Horse *was painted about 1840 by an unknown artist in Massachusetts. National Gallery of Art, Washington, D.C. Gift of Edgar William and Bernice Chrysler Garbisch* **389** *Semicircular hoops provide unusual base for this hobbyhorse* **390** *Leather horse and rider, c. 1880* **391** *Musician nods his head and moves his bow in mechanical music box, c. 1890*

Playthings & Pastimes

390

CHILDREN's TOYS mirror the tastes and trends of their times, and the toys of the early Colonial days in turn reflect the unfrivolous nature of that period. Very often there were no toys at all and imagination served to turn sticks and stones into games; children who lived along the seashore played with shells and pebbles. By the end of the seventeenth century, some English toys were being imported, but they were available to only a small fraction of the population. For the most part the early settlers fashioned crude playthings out of pine, oak, maple, and cherry wood from the forest.

The rocking horse, or hobbyhorse, was the most popular form of amusement for all children. Its design and construction presented a real challenge to the artisan—an opportunity to demonstrate imagination in contriving it from a single plank or shaping it sculpturally. Collectively, a group of hobbyhorses reveals the wide range of skills found among amateur craftsmen. The back and saddle of the horse required clever design for comfortable seating and the runners had to be sturdy enough for constant rocking over long periods. Realism in equine features was a matter of the toymaker's patience and ability; the lack of it in cruder models certainly did not hinder the child's fun. The plank forms, thin and elongated in their more economical construction, had the universal appeal of all primitive things. The more elaborate, full-bodied shapes approach carrousel figures of a later day and represent the handiwork of skilled carvers rather than amateur craftsmen. Hobbyhorses were forthright examples of folk carving and ingenuity, from the leather ears tacked into position to the genuine horsehair tails.

In New England villages the making of toys became a sideline for carvers and carpenters. In Pennsylvania German counties, where toymaking descended from the distinctive wood carving of the homeland, there was an abundance of charming miniatures—animals, birds, and other figures. Noah's Ark, with its full complement of paired birds and beasts, was particulary attractive to children. In addition there were the traditional Christmas decorations—the crèche and nativity scenes. Celebrated itinerants included the German carvers Wilhelm Schimmel and Aaron Mountz (often spelled Mounts) and the Swiss George Huguenin. Although Schimmel was especially noted for his birds, his most elaborate creation was the Garden of Eden, of which he made a number of copies. Here he stood Adam and Eve in the shade of a tree, surrounded them with a variety of animals, and enclosed the whole ensemble within a picket fence. He covered all this with heavy coats of whatever paint was available at the farmhouse, most often a barn red.

The wooden figures, although faithfully executed, still had one drawback: they lacked the animation so necessary to a child's sense of play. Out of this urgent need there developed other wooden toys, articulated with moving parts and mechanical arrangements of the simplest sort.

The vast variety of wooden toys included sets of miniature furniture with which to equip an entire dollhouse. There were chairs, tables, benches, stools, chests, beds, lowboys, and highboys. Some of these pieces, especially those made by a cabinetmaker for his children, are our finest examples of diminutive woodworking. Welsh dressers and corner cabinets provided display pieces in which to show off

391

392–398 *Diversity of approach to the design of a hobbyhorse is well illustrated in the examples shown. In 392 a log for the body is mounted on sticks. The fully rounded figure, 396, is carved from a single piece of pine. In 397 three layers of plank boards are put together with flattened results; the mane is cut in sawtooth fashion from the center plank*

392

393

394

395

the child's precious bits of miniature china and porcelain. An important addition to doll equipment was an American creation: the doll carriage. It came in every possible style and size and was usually a sideline of baby-carriage makers. Later on, in the second half of the nineteenth century, reed and wicker bodies replaced the wooden ones, which had been heavier and sturdier. The doll carriage was subjected to constant use and frequently handed down.

As tin toys followed those made of wood, in about 1840, a new realm opened up for the toy makers. Dies could easily stamp out all shapes and forms, which could then be crimped together at the seams for extra strength and rigidity. Mechanical playthings, a constant source of amusement for children, now also gained a new dimension. Though simple actions had been known as early as 1825, the

396

397

windup, or clockwork, toys with spring action came in with the popular wave of tin toys. These mechanisms could be installed to make a figure dance a jig, play an instrument, or—in the case of dolls—simply walk. They could produce locomotion in steam engines, paddle-wheelers, and fire trucks. Windup toys included capering clowns, music boxes, revolving tables on which monkeys danced, and a thousand and one novelties ideally suited to tin because of its lightness and the low cost of its manufacture. The present scarcity of tin toys from the seventies and eighties is incomprehensible when one remembers the record-breaking output of the toy makers in their heyday. One single manufacturer is known to

398

399

400

401

402   403

have produced forty million tin toys annually in the 1870s.

Fortunately for today's collectors, the cast-iron variety, which came in a bit later than tin, had a better chance for survival. Although cast-iron toys were indeed more solid, windup mechanisms were not suited to the heavier material, and vehicles equipped with wheels or rollers had to be pulled along by the child. In this category were the bell toys, which so delighted young children. The bell device was

most often attached to the axle of a cart or horse-drawn wagon and the bell chimed when the toy was in motion. Cast-iron pots, pans, and skillets were favored by young girls. Together with a miniature stove, these vessels completed a girl's kitchen equipment and could be used for baking cakes and cookies.

399–406 *Wheeled toys of many different types were favorites at the turn of the century. There were many animals mounted on platforms with wheels, engines and vehicles in great variety, coaches, wagons and omnibuses. Besides the cast-iron kinds to be pulled about, there were wind-up toys of tin, and the automobile, at first imported from Germany and France, was among these. Within a few years American toy autos were being made*

407

408 – 412

Dolls, Puppets & Marionettes

DOLLS, PUPPETS, and marionettes have always figured largely in the child's world of fantasy. Fortunately, their size and shape have not mattered, for in the early days of the Colonies the homemade dolls were crude indeed. One of the earliest, which was called—because of the obvious similarity—a bedpost doll, was simply a rounded stick with a face painted on it. In some regions children learned from friendly Indian tribes how to make simple puppets out of buckskin. But the universal favorites, on the farm and in the city, were rag dolls, which could be made by anybody who owned an extra bit of cloth; often a clothespin was used for the body. In an era of make-do they became cherished possessions.

The popularity of rag dolls eventually led to the manufacture of dolls in quantity. The pattern was made by stamping or printing a design on two separate pieces of cloth, one for the front and the other for the back. These were then cut out, sewn together, and stuffed.

Rag dolls were dressed in pieces of calico, muslin, linen, or silk left over from a dress or an appliqué bedspread. Occasionally a doll

might be clad in Quaker costume, but on the whole regional dress was not in evidence. There were, however, marked variations in doll construction, with cornhusks and nuthead dolls prevailing in rural areas.

Innovations constantly appeared on the doll market. In the 1870s a Yankee inventor named Joel Ellis came up with the mortise-and-tenon joint, by which wooden pieces could be inserted and fastened, or made movable. The practicability of these for doll construction led Ellis to the formation of a Vermont company for the manufacture of dolls that could assume all sorts of odd positions and perform acrobatic stunts. His success inspired the invention of the ball-and-socket joint for doll movements and many other improvements. After the walking doll came the talking doll, a by-product of Thomas Edison's work on the phonograph.

Puppets and marionettes have followed a very different pattern, since they are completely handmade, from the fashioning of the heads and facial expressions to the articulation of the figures and their costuming. Puppeteers make a clear distinction that sometimes comes as a surprise to the layman. In the true mean-

413

407 *Marionette Chinaman made to be operated by strings from a position above the stage. Head carved of black walnut and painted, costume of silk with rhinestone buttons, and papier-maché ball. Made by puppeteer Oliver Lano, c. 1870* **408–412** *Painted puppet heads of carved walnut. Wigs were made of fur and wool by Oliver Lano, c. 1870* **413** *Hand puppet, Judy, has stick in the body to hold up head. Painted wooden face and hands, velvet cap, and cotton clothing, c. 1870*

414   415   416

ing, puppets are manipulated directly by hand, or sometimes with a stick from underneath; marionettes are controlled by strings or wires from above. The puppeteer often conceives, writes, and directs the play, designs the stage and costumes, and creates all the sets and stage appurtenances in his own workshop. The miniature theater offers a rare form of self-expression in which artist, craftsman, stage director, and actor are combined in a single personality.

There have been few improvements in the technique of the puppet theater since Punch began his travels in England, almost three centuries ago. The methods of puppetry have a basic simplicity and honesty which do not encourage innovation. The stage is formed within a portable wooden framework which is covered with cloth or decorated alfresco. At the bottom edge of the stage opening, which generally comes just above the puppeteer's head, is a projecting shelf on which the properties may be placed. Sometimes there is a flap below the main opening out of which the devil may make a surprise appearance. Scenery is painted simply on cloth drops or board cutouts; for the purpose of the average Punch play a garden or any scene will serve. Furniture is not generally used. The gallows are set up by pegging the base of the gibbet into a hole in the shelf.

The puppets are hung upside down by loops in their skirts on a row of hooks inside the booth. The puppeteer plunges his hand into

414–419 *Marionettes as various characters in plays by the Lano family, well-known puppeteers, c. 1870. The Cannibal is shown in 417, and the Sultan's Choice, a fan dancer, in 419* **420, 421** *Puppets Punch and Judy, made by the Lano family, c. 1880*

417

418

419

420

421

422

423

424

425

426

427

428

429

the opening of the hollow costume, slips his index finger into the neck of the puppet, his thumb into one arm and his second finger into the other, and brings the figure onstage right side up. It is held at arm's length over his head.

Punch is always on the right hand and the other characters change on the left hand while Punch holds the attention of the audience. Sometimes extras, an army or a mob, are held up on a forked stick.

422–424 *The doll maker exercised much ingenuity in the construction of head and face when imported wax or bisque heads were unavailable. Cornhusks, nutheads, papier-maché, woven yarn, and stuffed cottons were a few of the materials pressed into service* **425, 426** *Pair of Indian dolls with carved wooden heads, stuffed bodies, and buckskin costumes. Made by Marie Rose of the Montana Cree Reservation* **427** *Rag doll Tilly, made about 1880* **428** *Negro doll with carved wooden head and stuffed body, made about 1870* **429** *Hand-painted doll's cradle, made in Pennsylvania, c. 1780*

430

A Penny Saved....

431

THRIFT WAS among the virtues that nineteenth-century parents tried to instill in their children. Every primer and Bible tract emphasized the value of saving a penny: "Resolve not to be poor; whatever you have, spend less and save more." "It is saving, not getting, that is the mother of riches," Benjamin Franklin had put it earlier. Proverbs and sermons of thrift at home or in Bible school were not entirely effective, however. It took the inventiveness of the small iron foundries to hit on a method of combining thrift with fun. Between 1850 and 1910, millions of mechanical banks were made by a handful of foundries.

Large copper pieces were first issued by the government in 1793; this led to improvised forms of the piggy bank made from gourds, clay, seashells, and some even whittled from wood. Such contrivances were followed by glass and china banks in a variety of shapes—houses, chickens, ducks, turkeys, wild and tame animals, public characters, and historic landmarks, including Plymouth Rock and the Liberty Bell.

By 1857, when the minting of large copper pennies was discontinued, manufacturers turned to the production of painted tin banks that looked like churches, gabled houses, drums, and bandboxes.

Just after the Civil War the first iron banks appeared. They were modeled after the square bank buildings, with a cupola and a "Savings Bank" inscription over the door. This plain bank building, unfortunately, offered little opportunity for novelty. Then the insertion of a simple spring action brought life into the still bank. Patent applications for the new designs have provided us with a record of the various types of mechanical banks. From about 1870, the intricate movements became increasingly popular, reaching a peak in sales before the close of the century. A single penny deposited in the slot brought a ticket of admission—a sideshow, a bit of amusement enjoyed by children and adults alike. The toy soldiers bowed, the mule kicked his heels, and the eagle flapped its wings. This approach to thrift proved more effective than stern admonitions and moralizing maxims.

430 *Cast-iron and polychromed Uncle Sam mechanical bank made its debut shortly after the Centennial Exhibition. It became one of the most popular toy banks of its day* **431** *A penny deposited brought the promise of action and a faint bark from the Speaking Dog bank, patented in 1885*

169

432

433

STUMP SPEAKER

170

434

435

436

432 *Spring action in the gun of William Tell sent the penny flying at the apple on the boy's head, 1896* **433** *Black Sambo characters were a product of the 1880s* **434** *For a penny the mule cart tipped upward, sending the mule into midair* **435** *Growing interest in baseball made this Dark Town Battery a favorite in its day, 1888* **436** *A coin is placed on the clown's hand, the lever is pressed in the back, and presto, the coin is swallowed* **437** *A cannon shoots the coin into the pylon of this Artillery Bank, 1892*

437

Less than a dozen firms produced these mechanical banks. A leader among them was the J. & E. Stevens Company, Cromwell, Connecticut, whose 1873 catalogue listed about two dozen distinct patterns. Other companies were located in Philadelphia and Lancaster, Pennsylvania; Kenton, Ohio; and Buffalo, New York. As each new volume or bit of research on this subject is completed, the total number of patterns increases. The latest count records about six hundred designs. The banks were manufactured in forms that

438

439

made up a veritable Noah's Ark, complete with frogs, turtles, rabbits, owls, pigs, horses, elephants, and lions. The American eagle feeding its young was a favorite. Others included a Punch and Judy theater, baseball batter and battery, the Old Woman Who Lived in the Shoe, a bowling alley, ping-pong players, fortunetellers, wood-choppers, and the like. Comic situations also had appeal: a boy being thrown by his mule or turning a somersault.

Current events played their part in influencing the choice of subjects. At the time of fairs and celebrations, such forms as Uncle Sam, the Liberty Bell, and Independence Hall were

438 Jonah banks his coins in the wide-open mouth of the whale, 1888 439 When the right forefoot is pressed, the frog's mouth opens wide to receive coin, 1872 440 The bear and hunter, in many versions, shoot the coin into a pouch for safekeeping, c. 1895 441 After coin deposit mule swings around to kick over watching boy 442 Organ Bank plays a tune as monkey doffs his hat and drops coin into slot 443 Trick Dog jumps through the hoop and lands coin in the barrel

440

produced by different foundries. Novelties were issued for special occasions, such as the Columbian World's Fair in 1892 and the Pan-American Exposition in 1901.

Although hardly an expression of folk art, the mechanical banks represent another field in which the patternmaker, molder, and colorist combined their talents to create articles of mass appeal.

441

ORGAN BANK

442

TRICK DOG

443

444

445

446

447

444 *The swinging acrobat provides the action in this mechanical bank, c. 1875* **445** *Punch and Judy bank provides action in the stage setting, 1884* **446** *Circus Elephant performs as follows: coin is placed between rings at lower right, ball held by acrobat at left is pulled back, clown turns at waist, and elephant's trunk flicks coin into slot, 1882* **447** *Figure in bank building turns to make deposit* **448** *Trick Pony takes coin in his mouth and bends his head to drop it into feedbox* **449** *The clown seated on a globe does a turn as coin is placed into slot* **450** *The miser holding bills waves his arms in this bank of very limited action, c. 1875*